# CONTENTS

## LECTURE V
## TAOISM



## LECTURE VI
## SOME CHINESE MANNERS AND CUSTOMS

# CHINA AND THE CHINESE

## THECHINESELANGUAGE

If the Chinese people were to file one by one past a given point, the interesting procession would never come to an end. Before the last man of those living to-day had gone by, another and a new generation would have grown up, and so on for ever and ever.

The importance, as a factor in the sum of human affairs, of this vast nation,—of its language, of its literature, of its religions, of its history, of its manners and customs,—goes therefore without saying. Yet a serious attention to China and her affairs is of very recent growth. Twenty-five years ago there was but one professor of Chinese in the United Kingdom of Great Britain and Ireland; and even that one spent his time more in adorning his profession than in imparting his knowledge to classes of eager students. Now there are all together five chairs of Chinese, the occupants of which are all more or less actively employed. But we are still sadly lacking in what Columbia University appears to have obtained by the stroke of a generous pen,—adequate funds for endowment. Meanwhile, I venture to offer my respectful congratulations to Columbia University on having surmounted this initial difficulty, and also to prophesy that the foresight of the liberal donor will be amply justified before many years are over.

I have often been asked if Chinese is, or is not, a difficult language to learn. To this question it is quite impossible to give a categorical answer, for the simple reason that Chinese consists of at least two languages, one colloquial and the other written, which for all practical purposes are about as distinct as they well could be.

Colloquial Chinese is a comparatively easy matter. It is, in fact, more easily acquired in the early stages than colloquial French or German. A student will begin to speak from the very first, for the simple reason that there is no other way. There are no Declensions or Conjugations to be learned, and consequently no Paradigms or Irregular Verbs.

In a day or two the student should be able to say a few simple things. After three months he should be able to deal with his ordinary requirements; and after six months he should be able to chatter away more or less accurately on a variety of interesting subjects. A great deal depends upon the method by which he is taught.

The written or book language, on the other hand, may fairly be regarded as a sufficient study for a lifetime; not because of the peculiar script, which yields when systematically attacked, but because the style of the book language is often so extremely terse as to make it obscure, and sometimes so lavishly ornate that without wide reading it is not easy to follow the figurative phraseology, and historical and mythological allusions, which confront one on every page.

There are plenty of men, and some women, nowadays, who can carry on a conversation in Chinese with the utmost facility, and even with grace. Some speak so well as to be practically indistinguishable from Chinamen.

There are comparatively few men, and I venture to say still fewer, if any, women, who can read an ordinary Chinese book with ease, or write an ordinary Chinese letter at all.

Speaking of women as students of Chinese, there have been so far only two who have really placed themselves in the front rank. It gives me great pleasure to add that both these ladies, lady missionaries, were natives of America, and that it was my privilege while in China to know them both. In my early studies of Chinese I received much advice and assistance from one of them, the late Miss Lydia Fay. Later on, I came to entertain a high respect for the scholarship and literary attainments of Miss Adèle M. Fielde, a well-known authoress.

Before starting upon a course of colloquial Chinese, it is necessary for the student to consider in what part of China he proposes to put his knowledge into practice. If he intends to settle or do business in Peking, it is absolute waste of time for him to learn the dialect of Shanghai. Theoretically, there is but one language spoken by the Chinese people in China proper,—over an area of some two million square miles, say twenty-five times the area of England and Scotland together. Practically, there are about eight well-marked dialects, all clearly of a common stock, but so distinct as to constitute eight different languages, any two of which are quite as unlike as English and Dutch.

These dialects may be said to fringe the coast line of the Empire of China. Starting from Canton and coasting northward, before we have left behind us the province in which Canton is situated, Kuangtung, we reach Swatow, where a totally new dialect is spoken. A short run now brings us to Amoy, the dialect of which, though somewhat resembling that of Swatow, is still very different in many respects. Our next stage is Foochow, which is in the same province as Amoy, but possesses a special dialect of its own. Then on to Wênchow, with another dialect, and so on to Ningpo with yet another, widely spoken also in Shanghai, though the latter place really has a *patois* of its own.

Farther north to Chefoo, and thence to Peking, we come at last into the range of the great dialect, popularly known as Mandarin, which sweeps round behind the narrow strip of coast occupied by the various dialects above mentioned, and dominates a hinterland constituting about four-fifths of China proper. It is obvious, then, that for a person who settles in a coast district, the dialect of that district must be his chief care, while for the traveller and explorer Mandarin will probably stand him in best stead.

The dialect of Peking is now regarded as standard "Mandarin"; but previous to the year 1425 the capital was at Nanking, and the dialect of Nanking was the Mandarin then in vogue. Consequently, Pekingese is the language which all Chinese officials are now bound to speak.

Those who come from certain parts of the vast hinterland speak Mandarin almost as a mother tongue, while those from the seaboard and certain adjacent parts of the interior have nearly as much difficulty in acquiring it, and quite as much difficulty in speaking it with a correct accent, as the average foreigner.

The importance of Mandarin, the "official language" as the Chinese call it, is beyond question. It is the vehicle of oral communication between all Chinese officials, even in cases where they come from the same part of the country and speak the same *patois*, between officials and their servants, between judge and prisoner. Thus, in every court of justice throughout the Empire the proceedings are carried on in Mandarin, although none of the parties to the case may understand a single word. The prosecutor, on his knees, tells his story in his native dialect. This story is rendered into Mandarin by an official interpreter for the benefit of the magistrate; the magistrate asks his questions or makes his remarks in Mandarin, and these are translated into the local dialect for the benefit of the litigants. Even if the magistrate knows the dialect himself,—as is often the case, although no magistrate may hold office in his own province,—still it is not strictly permissible for him to make use of the local dialect for magisterial purposes.

It may be added that in all large centres, such as Canton, Foochow, and Amoy, there will be found, among the well-to-do tradesmen and merchants, many who can make themselves intelligible in something which approximates to the dialect of Peking, not to mention that two out of the above three cities are garrisoned by Manchu troops, who of course speak that dialect as their native tongue.

Such is Mandarin. It may be compared to a limited extent with Urdu, the camp language of India. It is obviously the form of colloquial which should be studied by all, except those who have special interests in special districts, in which case, of course, the *patois* of the locality comes to the front.

We will now suppose that the student has made up his mind to learn Mandarin. The most natural thing for him, then, to do will be to look around him for a grammar. He may have trouble in finding one. Such works do actually exist, and they have been, for the most part, to quote a familiar trade-mark, "made in Germany." They are certainly not made by the Chinese, who do not possess, and never have possessed, in their language, an equivalent term for grammar. The language is quite beyond reach of the application of such rules as have been successfully deduced from Latin and Greek.

The Chinese seem always to have spoken in monosyllables, and these monosyllables seem always to have been incapable of inflection, agglutination, or change of any kind. They are in reality root-ideas, and are capable of adapting themselves to their surroundings, and of playing each one such varied parts as noun, verb (transitive, neuter, or even causal), adverb, and conjunction.

The word 我 *wo*, which for convenience' sake I call "I," must be rendered into English by "me" whenever it is the object of some other word, which, also for convenience' sake, I call a verb. It has further such extended senses as "egoistic" and "subjective."

For example: 我爱他 *wo ai t'a*.

The first of these characters, which is really the root-idea of "self," stands here for the pronoun of the first person; the last, which is really the root-idea of "not self," "other," stands for the pronoun of the third person; and the middle character for the root-idea of "love."

This might mean in English, "I love him," or "I love her," or "I love it,"—for there is no gender in Chinese, any more than there is any other indication of grammatical susceptibilities. We can only decide if "him," "her," or "it" is intended by the context, or by the circumstances of the case.

Now if we were to transpose what I must still call the pronouns, although they are not pronouns except when we make them so, we should have—

他爱我 *t'a ai wo*

"he, she, *or* it loves me," the only change which the Chinese words have undergone being one of position; while in English, in addition to the inflection of the pronouns, the "love" of the first person becomes "loves" in the third person.

Again, supposing we wished to write down—

"People love him (or her),"

we should have—

人爱他 *jen ai t'a,*

in which once more the noticeable feature is that the middle character, although passing from the singular to the plural number, suffers no change of any kind whatever.

Further, the character for "man" is in the plural simply because such a rendering is the only one which the genius of the Chinese language will here tolerate, helped out by the fact that the word by itself does not mean "*a* man," but rather what we may call the root-idea of humanity.

Such terms as "a man," or "six men," or "some men," or "many men," would be expressed each in its own particular way.

"All men," for instance, would involve merely the duplication of the character *jen:*—

人人爱他 *jen jen ai t'a.*

It is the same with tenses in Chinese. They are not brought out by inflection, but by the use of additional words.

来 *lai* is the root-idea of "coming," and lends itself as follows to the exigencies of conjugation:—

Standing alone, it is imperative:—

来 *Lai!* = "come!" "here!"

我来 *wo lai* = "I come, *or* am coming."

他来 *t'a lai* = "he comes, *or* is coming."

And by inserting 不 *pu*, a root-idea of negation,—

他不来 *t'a pu lai* = "he comes not, *or* is not coming."

To express an interrogative, we say,—

他来不来 *t'a lai pu lai* = "he come no come?" *i.e.* "is he coming?"

submitting the two alternatives for the person addressed to choose from in reply.

The indefinite past tense is formed by adding the word 了 *liao* or *lo* "finished":—

他来了 *t'a lai lo* = "he come finish," = "he has come."

This may be turned into the definite past tense by inserting some indication of time; *e.g.*

他早上来了 = "he came this morning."

Here we see that the same words may be indefinite or definite according to circumstances.

It is perhaps more startling to find that the same words may be both active and passive.

Thus, 丢 *tiu* is the root-idea of "loss," "to lose," and 了 puts it into the past tense.

Now 我丢了 means, and can only mean, "I have lost"—something understood, or to be expressed. Strike out 我 and substitute 書 "a book." No Chinaman would think that the new sentence meant "The book has lost"—something understood, or to be expressed, as for instance its cover; but he would grasp at once the real sense, "The book is or has been lost."

In the case of such, a phrase as "The book has lost" its cover, quite a different word would be used for "lost."

We have the same phenomenon in English. In the *New York Times* of February 13, I read, "Mr. So-and-so dined," meaning not that Mr. So-and-so took his dinner, but had been entertained at dinner by a party of friends,—a neuter verb transformed into a passive verb by the logic of circumstances.

By a like process the word 死 *ssŭ* "to die" may also mean "to make to die" = "to kill."

The word 金 *chin* which stands for "gold" as a substantive may also stand, as in English, for an adjective, and for a verb, "to gold," *i.e.* to regard as gold, to value highly.

There is nothing in Chinese like love, loving, lovely, as noun substantive, verb, and adverb. The word, written or spoken, remains invariably, so far as its own economy is concerned, the same. Its function in a sentence is governed entirely by position and by the influence of other words upon it, coupled with the inexorable logic of attendant circumstances.

When a Chinaman comes up to you and says, "You wantchee my, no wantchee," he is doing no foolish thing, at any rate from his own point of view. To save himself the trouble of learning grammatical English, he is taking the language and divesting it of all troublesome inflections, until he has at his control a set of root-ideas, with which he can juggle as in his own tongue. In other words, "you wantchee my, no wantchee," is nothing more nor less than literally rendered Chinese:—

你要我不要 *ni yao wo, pu yao* = do you want me or not?

In this "pidgin" English he can express himself as in Chinese by merely changing the positions of the words:—

"He wantchee my." "My wantchee he."

"My belong Englishman."

"That knife belong my."

Some years back, when I was leaving China for England with young children, their faithful Chinese nurse kept on repeating to the little ones the following remarkable sentence, "My too muchey solly you go steamah; you no solly my."

All this is very absurd, no doubt; still it is *bona fide* Chinese, and illustrates very forcibly how an intelligible language may be constructed of root-ideas arranged in logical sequence.

If the last word had now been said in reference to colloquial, it would be as easy for us to learn to speak Chinese as it is for a Chinaman to learn to speak Pidgin-English. There is, however, a great obstacle still in the way of the student. The Chinese language is peculiarly lacking in vocables; that is to say, it possesses very few sounds for the conveyance of speech. The dialect of Peking is restricted to four hundred and twenty, and as every word in the language must fall under one or other of those sounds, it follows that if there are 42,000 words in the language (and the standard dictionary contains 44,000), there is an average of 100 words to each sound. Of course, if any sound had less than 100 words attached to it, some other sound would have proportionately more. Thus, accepting the average, we should have 100 things or ideas, all expressed in speech, for instance, by the one single sound *I*.

The confusion likely to arise from such conditions needs not to be enlarged upon; it is at once obvious, and probably gave rise to the following sapient remark by a globe-trotting author, which I took from a newspaper in England:—

"In China, the letter *I* has one hundred and forty-five different ways of being pronounced, and each pronunciation has a different meaning."

It would be difficult to squeeze more misleading nonsense into a smaller compass. Imagine the agonies of a Chinese infant school, struggling with the letter *I* pronounced in 145 different ways, with a different meaning to each! It will suffice to say, what everybody here present must know, that Chinese is not in any sense an alphabetic language, and that consequently there can be no such thing as "the letter *I*."

When closely examined, this great difficulty of many words with but one common sound melts rapidly away, until there is but a fairly small residuum with which the student has to contend. The same difficulty confronts us, to a slighter extent, even in English. If I say, "I met a bore in Broadway," I may mean one of several things. I may mean a tidal wave, which is at once put out of court by the logic of circumstances. Or I may mean a wild animal, which also has circumstances against it.

To return to Chinese. In the first place, although there are no doubt 42,000 separate written characters in the Chinese language, about one-tenth of that number, 4200, would more than suffice for the needs of an average speaker. Adopting this scale, we have 420 sounds and 4200 words, or ten words to each sound,—still a sufficient hindrance to anything like certain intelligibility of speech. But this is not the whole case. The ten characters, for instance, under each sound, are distributed over four separate groups, formed by certain modulations of the voice, known as Tones, so that actually there would be only an average of 2-1/2 words liable to absolute confusion. Thus 烟 yen[1] means "smoke"; 鹽 yen[2] means "salt"; 眼 yen[3] means "an eye"; and 雁 yen[4] means "a goose."

These modulations are not readily distinguished at first; but the ear is easily trained, and it soon becomes difficult to mistake them.

Nor is this all. The Chinese, although their language is monosyllabic, do not make an extensive use of monosyllables in speech to express a single thing or idea. They couple their words in pairs.

Thus, for "eye" they would say, not *yen*, which strictly means "hole," or "socket," but *yen ching*, the added word *ching*, which means "eyeball," tying down the term to the application required, namely, "eye."

In like manner it is not customary to talk about *yen*, "salt," as we do, but to restrict the term as required in each case by the addition of some explanatory word; for instance, 白盐 "white salt," *i.e.* "table salt"; 黑盐 "black salt," *i.e.* "coarse salt"; all of which tends very much to prevent confusion with other words pronounced in the same tone.

There are also certain words used as suffixes, which help to separate terms which might otherwise be confused. Thus 裹 *kuo*[3] means "to wrap," and 果 *kuo*[3] means "fruit," the two being identical in sound and tone. And *yao kuo* might mean either "I want fruit" or "I want to wrap." No one, however, says *kuo* for "fruit," but *kuo tzŭ*. The suffix *tzŭ* renders confusion impossible.

Of course there is no confusion in reading a book, where each thing or idea, although of the same sound and tone, is represented by a different symbol.

On the whole, it may be said that misconceptions in the colloquial are not altogether due to the fact that the Chinese language is poorly provided with sounds. Many persons, otherwise gifted, are quite unable to learn any foreign tongue.

Let us now turn to the machinery by means of which the Chinese arrest the winged words of speech, and give to mere thought and utterance a more concrete and a more lasting form.

The written language has one advantage over the colloquial: it is uniformly the same all over China; and the same document is equally intelligible to natives of Peking and Canton, just as the Arabic and Roman numerals are understood all over Europe, although pronounced differently by various nations.

To this fact some have attributed the stability of the Chinese Empire and the permanence of her political and social institutions.

If we take the written language of to-day, which is to all intents and purposes the written language of twenty-five hundred years ago, we gaze at first on what seems to be a confused mass of separate signs, each sign being apparently a fortuitous concourse of dots and dashes. Gradually, however, the eye comes to perceive that every now and again there is to be found in one character a certain portion which has already been observed in another, and this may well have given rise to the idea that each character is built up of parts equivalent to our letters of the alphabet. These portions are of two kinds, and must be considered under two separate heads.

Under the first head come a variety of words, which also occur as substantive characters, such as dog, vegetation, tree, disease, metal, words, fish, bird, man, woman. These are found to indicate the direction in which the sense of the whole character is to be sought.

Thus, whenever 犭 "dog" occurs in a character, the reader may prepare for the name of some animal, as for instance 狮 *shih* "lion," 猫 *mao* "cat," 狼 *lang* "wolf", 猪 *ehu* "pig."

Two of these are interesting words. (1) There are no lions in China; *shih* is merely an imitation of the Persian word *shír*. (2) *Mao*, the term for a "cat," is obviously an example of onomatopoeia.

The character 犭 will also indicate in many cases such attributes as 猾 *hua* "tricky," 狠 *hên*, "aggressive," 猛 *mêng* "fierce," and other characteristics of animals.

Similarly, 艹 *ts'ao* "vegetation" will hint at some plant; *e.g.* 草 *ts'ao* "grass," 荷 *ho* "the lily," 芝 *chih* "the plant of immortality."

木 *mu* "a tree" usually points toward some species of tree; *e.g.* 松 *sung* "a fir tree," 桑 *sang* "a mulberry tree"; and by extension it points toward anything of wood, as 板 *pan* "a board," 桌 *cho* "a table," 椅 *i* "a chair," and so on.

So 魚 *yü* "a fish" and 鸟 鳥 *niao* "a bird" are found in all characters of ichthyological or ornithological types, respectively.

人 *jen* "a man" is found in a large number of characters dealing with humanity under varied aspects; *e.g.* 你 *ni* "thou," 他 *t'a* "he," 作 *tso* "to make," 仗 *chang* "a weapon," 傑 *chieh* "a hero," 儒 *ju* "a scholar," "a Confucianist"; while it has been pointed out that such words as 奸 *chien* "treacherous," 媚 *mei* "to flatter," and 妒 *tu* "jealousy," are all written with the indicator 女 *nü* "woman" at the side.

The question now arises how these significant parts got into their present position. Have they always been there, and was the script artificially constructed off-hand, as is the case with Mongolian and Manchu? The answer to this question can hardly be presented in a few words, but involves the following considerations.

It seems to be quite certain that in very early times, when the possibility and advantage of committing thought to writing first suggested themselves to the Chinese mind, rude pictures of *things* formed the whole stock in trade. Such were

Sun, moon, mountains, hand, child, wood, bending official, mouth, ox, and claws.

in many of which it is not difficult to trace the modern forms of to-day,

日 月 山 手 子 木 臣 口 牛 爪

It may here be noted that there was a tendency to curves so long as the characters were scratched on bamboo tablets with a metal stylus. With the invention of paper in the first century A.D., and the substitution of a hair-pencil for the stylus, verticals and horizontals came more into vogue.

The second step was the combination of two pictures to make a third; for instance, a mouth with something coming out of it is "the tongue," 舌; a mouth with something else coming out of it is "speech," "words," 言; two trees put side by side make the picture of a "forest," 林.

The next step was to produce pictures of ideas. For instance, there already existed in speech a word *ming*, meaning "bright." To express this, the Chinese placed in juxtaposition the two brightest things known to them. Thus 日 the "sun" and 月 the "moon" were combined to form 明 *ming* "bright." There is as yet no suggestion of phonetic influence. The combined character has a sound quite different from that of either of its component parts, which are *jih* and *yüeh* respectively.

In like manner, 日 "sun" and 木 "tree," combined as 東, "the sun seen rising through trees," signified "the east"; 言 "words" and 舌 "tongue" = 話 "speech"; 友 (old form 㕛) "two hands" = "friendship"; 女 "woman" and 子 "child" = 好 "good"; 女 "woman" and 生 "birth," "born of a woman" = 姓 "clan name," showing that the ancient Chinese traced through the mother and not through the father; 勿 streamers used in signalling a negative = "do not!"

From 林 "two trees," the picture of a forest, we come to 森 "three trees," suggesting the idea of density of growth and darkness; 孝 "a child at the feet of an old man" = "filial piety"; 戈 "a spear" and 手 "to kill," suggesting the defensive attitude of individuals in primeval times = 我 "I, me"; 我 "I, my," and 羊 "sheep," suggesting the obligation to respect another man's flocks = 義 "duty toward one's neighbour"; 大 "large" and 羊 "sheep" = 美 "beautiful"; and 善, "virtuous," also has "sheep" as a component part,—why we do not very satisfactorily make out, except that of course the sheep would play an important rôle among early pastoral tribes. The idea conveyed by what we call the conjunction "and" is expressed in Chinese by an ideogram, viz. 及, which was originally the picture of a hand, seizing what might be the tail of the coat of a man preceding, *scilicet* following.

The third and greatest step in the art of writing was reached when the Chinese, who had been trying to make one character do for several similar-sounding words of different meanings, suddenly bethought themselves of distinguishing these several similar-sounding words by adding to the original character employed some other character indicative of the special sense in which each was to be understood. Thus, in speech the sound *ting* meant "the sting of an insect," and was appropriately pictured by what is now written 丁.

There were, however, other words also expressed by the sound *ting*, such as "a boil," "the top or tip," "to command," "a nail," "an ingot," and "to arrange." These would be distinguished in speech by the tones and suffixes, as already described; but in writing, if 丁 were used for all alike, confusion would of necessity arise. To remedy this, it occurred to some one in very early ages to make 丁, and other similar pictures of things or ideas, serve as what we now call Phonetics, *i.e.* the part which suggests the sound of the character, and to add in each case an indicator of the special sense intended to be conveyed. Thus, taking 丁 as the phonetic base, in order to express *ting*, "a boil," the indicator for "disease," 疒, was added, making 疔; for *ting*, "the top," the indicator for "head," 页, was added, making 顶; for "to command," the symbol for "mouth," 口 was added, making 叮; for "nail," and also for "ingot," the symbol for "metal," 金, was added, making 釘; and for "to arrange," the symbol for "speech," 言, was added, making 訂. We thus obtain five new words, which, so far as the written language is concerned, are easily distinguishable one from another, namely, *ting* "a sting," disease-*ting* = "a boil," head-*ting* = "the top," mouth-*ting* = "to command," metal-*ting* = "a nail," speech-*ting* = "to arrange." In like manner, the words for "mouth," "to rap," and "a button," were all pronounced *k'ou*. Having got 口 *k'ou* as the picture of a mouth, that was taken as the phonetic base, and to express "to rap," the symbol for "hand," 手 or 扌, was added, making 扣; while to express "button," the symbol for "metal," 金 was added, making 釦. So that we have *k'ou* = "mouth," hand-*k'ou* = "to rap," and metal-*k'ou* = "button."

Let us take a picture of an idea. We have 東 *tung* = the sun seen through the trees,—"the east." When the early Chinese wished to write down *tung* "to freeze," they simply took the already existing 東 as the phonetic base, and added to it "an icicle," 冫, thus 凍. And when they wanted to write down *tung* "a beam," instead of "icicle," they put the obvious indicator 木 "wood," thus 棟.

We have now got the two portions into which the vast majority of Chinese characters can be easily resolved.

There is first the phonetic base, itself a character originally intended to represent some thing or idea, and then borrowed to represent other things and ideas similarly pronounced; and secondly, the indicator, another character added to the phonetic base in order to distinguish between the various things and ideas for which the same phonetic base was used.

All characters, however, do not yield at once to the application of our rule. 要 *yao* "to will, to want," is composed of 西 "west" and 女 "woman." What has western woman to do with the sign of the future? In the days before writing, the

Chinese called the waist of the body *yao*. By and by they wrote 要, a rude picture of man with his arms akimbo and his legs crossed, thus accentuating the narrower portion, the waist. Then, when it was necessary to write down *yao*, "to will," they simply borrowed the already existing word for "waist." In later times, when writing became more exact, they took the indicator 月 "flesh," and added it wherever the idea of waist had to be conveyed. And thus 腰 it is still written, while *yao*, "to will, to want," has usurped the character originally invented for "waist."

In some of their own identifications native Chinese scholars have often shown themselves hopelessly at sea. For instance, 天 "the sky," figuratively God, was explained by the first Chinese lexicographer, whose work has come down to us from about one hundred years after the Christian era, as composed of 一 "one" and 大 "great," the "one great" thing; whereas it was simply, under its oldest form, 𠀘, a rude anthropomorphic picture of the Deity.

Even the early Jesuit Fathers of the seventeenth and eighteenth centuries, to whom we owe so much for pioneer work in the domain of Sinology, were not without occasional lapses of the kind, due no doubt to a laudable if excessive zeal. Finding the character 船, which is the common word for "a ship," as indicated by 舟, the earlier picture-character for "boat" seen on the left-hand side, one ingenious Father proceeded to analyse it as follows:—

> 舟 "ship," 八 "eight," 口 "mouth" = eight mouths on a ship—"the Ark."

But the right-hand portion is merely the phonetic of the character; it was originally 铅 "lead," which gave the sound required; then the indicator "boat" was substituted for "metal."

So with the word 禁 "to prohibit." Because it could be analysed into two 木木 "trees" and 示 "a divine proclamation," an allusion was discovered therein to the two trees and the proclamation of the Garden of Eden; whereas again the proper analysis is into indicator and phonetic.

Nor is such misplaced ingenuity confined to the Roman Catholic Church. In 1892 a Protestant missionary published and circulated broadcast what he said was "evidence in favour of the Gospels," being nothing less than a prophecy of Christ's coming hidden in the Chinese character 來 "to come." He pointed out that this was composed of 十 "a cross," with two 人人 'men,' one on each side, and a 'greater man' 人 in the middle.

That analysis is all very well for the character as it stands now; but before the Christian era this same character was written 來 and was a picture, not of men and of a cross, but of a sheaf of corn. It came to mean "come," says the Chinese etymologist, "because corn *comes* from heaven."

Such is the written language of China, and such indeed it was, already under the dominion of the phonetic system, by which endless new combinations may still be formed, at the very earliest point to which history, as distinguished from legend, will carry us,—some eight or nine centuries B.C. There are no genuine remains of pure picture-writing, to enable us to judge how far the Chinese had got before the phonetic system was invented, though many attempts have been made to palm off gross forgeries as such.

The great majority of characters, as I have said, are capable of being easily resolved into the two important parts which I have attempted to describe—the original phonetic portion, which guides toward pronunciation, and the added indicator, which guides toward the sense.

Even the practical student, who desires to learn to read and write Chinese for purely business purposes, will find himself constrained to follow out this analysis, if he wishes to commit to memory a serviceable number of characters. With no other hold upon them beyond their mere outlines, he will find the characters so bewildering, so elusive, as to present almost insuperable difficulties.

But under the influence of systematic study, coupled with a fair amount of perseverance, these difficulties disappear, and leave the triumphant student amply rewarded for his pains.

# A CHINESE LIBRARY

The endowment of a Chinese chair at Columbia University naturally suggests the acquisition of a good Chinese library. At the University of Cambridge, England, there is what I can only characterise as an ideal Chinese library. It was not bought off-hand in the market,—such a collection indeed would never come into the market,—but the books were patiently and carefully brought together by my predecessor in the Chinese chair during a period of over forty years' residence in China. The result is an admirable selection of representative works, always in good, and sometimes in rare, editions, covering the whole field of what is most valuable in Chinese literature.

I now propose, with your approval, to give a slight sketch of the Cambridge Library, in which I spend a portion of almost every day of my life, and which I further venture to recommend as the type of that collection which Columbia University should endeavour to place upon her shelves.

The Chinese library at Cambridge consists of 4304 volumes, roughly distributed under seven heads. These volumes, it should be stated, are not the usual thin, paper-covered volumes of an ordinary Chinese work, but they consist each of several of the original Chinese volumes bound together in cloth or leather, lettered on the back, and standing on the shelves, as our books do, instead of lying flat, as is the custom in China.

Division A contains, first of all, the Confucian Canon, which now consists of nine separate works.

There is the mystic *Book of Changes*, that is to say, the eight changes or combinations which can be produced by a line and a broken line, either one of which is repeated twice with the other, or three times by itself.

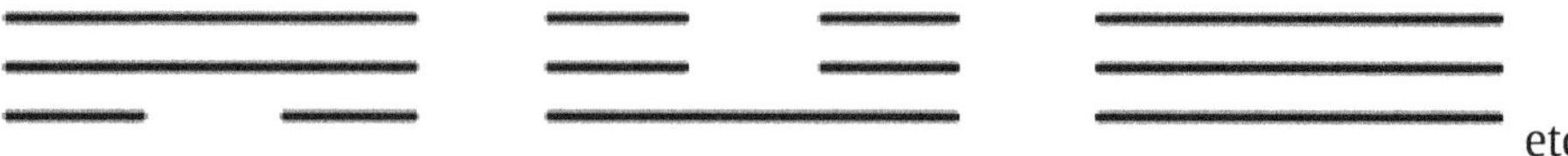

These trigrams are said to have been copied from the back of a tortoise by an ancient monarch, who doubled them into hexagrams, and so increased the combinations to sixty-four, each one of which represents some active or passive power in nature.

Confucius said that if he could devote fifty years to the study of this work, he might come to be without great faults; but neither native nor foreign scholars can really make anything out of it. Some regard it as a Book of Fate. One erratic genius of the West has gone so far as to say that it is only a vocabulary of the language of some old Central Asian tribe.

We are on somewhat firmer ground with the *Book of History*, which is a collection of very ancient historical documents, going back twenty centuries B.C., arranged and edited by Confucius. These documents, mere fragments as they are, give us glimpses of China's early civilisation, centuries before the historical period, to which we shall come later on, can fairly be said to begin.

Then we have the *Book of Odes*, consisting of some three hundred ballads, also rescued by Confucius from oblivion, on which as a basis the great superstructure of modern Chinese poetry has been raised.

Next comes an historical work by Confucius, known as the *Spring and Autumn*: it should be Springs and Autumns, for the title refers to the yearly records, to the annals, in fact, of the native State of Confucius himself.

The fifth in the series is the *Book of Rites*. This deals, as its title indicates, with ceremonial, and contains an infinite number of rules for the guidance of personal conduct under a variety of conditions and circumstances. It was compiled at a comparatively late date, the close of the second century B.C., and scarcely ranks in authority with the other four.

The above are called the Five Classics; they were for many centuries six in number, a *Book of Music* being included, and they were engraved on forty-six huge stone tablets about the year 170 A.D. Only mutilated portions of these tablets still remain.

The other four works which make up the Confucian Canon are known as the Four Books. They consist of a short moral treatise entitled the *Great Learning*, or Learning for Adults; the *Doctrine of the Mean*, another short philosophical treatise; the *Analects*, or conversations of Confucius with his disciples, and other details of the sage's daily life; and lastly, similar conversations of Mencius with his disciples and with various feudal nobles who sought his advice.

These nine works are practically learned by heart by the Chinese undergraduate. But there are in addition many commentaries and exegetical works—the best of which stand in the Cambridge Library—designed to elucidate the true purport of the Canon; and these must also be studied. They range from the commentary of K'ung An-kuo of the second century B.C., a descendant of Confucius in the twelfth degree, down to that of Yüan Yüan, a well-known scholar who only died so recently as 1849. These commentaries include both of the two great schools of interpretation, the earlier of which was accepted until the twelfth century A.D., when it was set aside by China's most brilliant scholar, Chu Hsi, who substituted the interpretation still in vogue, and obligatory at the public competitive examinations which admit to an official career.

Archæological works referring to the Canon have been published in great numbers. The very first book in our Catalogue is an account of every article mentioned in these old records, accompanied in all cases by woodcuts. Thus the foreign student may see not only the robes and caps in which ancient worthies of the Confucian epoch appeared, but their chariots, their banners, their weapons, and general paraphernalia of everyday life.

Side by side with the sacred books of Confucianism stand the heterodox writings of the Taoist philosophers, the nominal founder of which school, known as Lao Tzŭ, flourished at an unknown date before Confucius. Some of these are deeply interesting; others have not escaped the suspicion of forgery—a suspicion which attaches more or less to any works produced before the famous Burning of the Books, in B.C. 211, from which the Confucian Canon was preserved almost by a miracle. An Emperor at that date made an attempt to destroy all literature, so that a fresh start might be made from himself.

But I do not intend to detain you at present over Taoism, about which I hope to say more on a subsequent occasion. Still less shall I have anything to say on the few Buddhist works which are also to be found in the

Cambridge collection. It is rather along less well-beaten paths that I shall ask you to accompany me now.

In Division B, the first thing which catches the eye is a long line of 217 thick volumes, about a foot in height. These are the dynastic histories of China, in a uniform edition published in the year 1747, under the auspices of the famous Emperor Ch'ien Lung, who himself contributed a Preface.

The first of this series, known as *The Historical Record*, was produced by a very remarkable man, named Ssŭ-ma Ch'ien, sometimes called the Father of History, the Herodotus of China, who died nearly one hundred years B.C.; and over his most notable work it may not be unprofitable to linger awhile.

Starting with the five legendary Emperors, some 2700 years B.C., the historian begins by giving the annals of each reign under the various more or less legendary dynasties which succeeded, and thence onward right down to his own times, the last five or six hundred years, *i.e.* from about 700 B.C., belonging to a genuinely historical period. These annals form Part I of the five parts into which the historian divides his scheme.

Part II is occupied by chronological tables of the Emperors and their reigns, of the suzerains and vassal nobles under the feudal system which was introduced about 1100 B.C., and also of the nobles created to form an aristocracy after the feudal system had been swept away and replaced by the old Imperial rule, about 200 B.C.

Part III consists of eight important and interesting chapters: (1) on the Rites and Ceremonies of the period covered, (2) on Music, (3) on the Pitch-pipes, a series of twelve bamboo tubes of varying lengths, the notes from which were supposed to be bound up in some mysterious way with the good and bad fortunes of mankind, (4) on the Calendar, (5) on the Stars, (6) on the Imperial Sacrifices to Heaven and Earth, (7) on the Waterways of the Empire, and lastly (8) on Commerce, Coinage, etc.

Part IV deals with the reigns, so to speak, of the vassal nobles under the feudal system, the reigns of the suzerains having been already included in Part I.

Part V consists of biographies of the most eminent men who came to the front during the whole period covered.

These biographies are by no means confined to virtuous statesmen or heroic generals, as we might very reasonably have expected. The Chinese historian took a much broader view of his responsibilities to future ages, and along with the above virtuous statesmen and heroic generals he included lives of famous assassins, of tyrannical officials, of courtiers, of flatterers, of men with nothing beyond the gift of the gab, of politicians, of fortune-tellers, and the like.

This principle seems now to be widely recognised in the compilation of biographical collections. It was initiated by a Chinese historian one hundred years B.C.

His great work has come down to us as near as possible intact. To the Chinese it is, and always has been, a priceless treasure; so much so that every succeeding Dynastic History has been modelled pretty much upon the same lines.

The custom has always been for the incoming dynasty to issue the history of the dynasty it has overthrown, based upon materials which have been gathered daily during the latter's lease of power. At this moment the Historiographer's Department in Peking should be noting down current events for the use of posterity, in the established belief that all dynasties, even the most powerful, come to an end some day.

In addition to the Dynastic History proper, a custom has grown up of compiling what is called the "Veritable Record" of the life of the reigning Emperor. This is supposed to be written up every day, and with an absolute fidelity which it is unnecessary to suspect, since the Emperors are never allowed under any circumstances to cast an eye over their own records.

When the Hanlin College was burnt down, in 1900, some said that the "Veritable Records" of the present dynasty were destroyed. Others alleged that they had been carted away several days previously. However this may be, the "Veritable Records" of the great Ming dynasty, which came to a close in 1644, after three hundred years of power, are safe in Division B of the Cambridge Library, filling eighty-four large volumes of manuscript.

The next historical epoch is that of Ssŭ-ma Kuang, a leading statesman and scholar of the eleventh century A.D., who, after nineteen years of continuous labour, produced a general history of China, in the form of a chronological narrative, beginning with the fourth century B.C. and ending with the middle of the tenth century A.D. This work, which is popularly known as *The Mirror of History,* and is quite independent of the dynastic histories, fills thirty-three of our large bound-up volumes.

There is a quaint passage in the old man's Preface, dated 1084, and addressed to the Emperor:—

"Your servant's physical strength is now relaxed; his eyes are short-sighted and dim; of his teeth but a few remain. His memory is so impaired that the events of the moment are forgotten as he turns away from them, his energies having been wholly exhausted in the production of this book. He therefore hopes that your Majesty will pardon his vain attempt for the sake of his loyal intention, and in moments of leisure will deign to cast the Sacred Glance over this work, so as to learn from the rise and fall of former dynasties the secret of the successes and failures of the present hour. Then, if such knowledge shall be applied for the advantage of the Empire, even though your servant may lay his bones in the Yellow Springs, the aim and ambition of his life will be fulfilled."

Biography, as we have already seen, is to some extent provided for under the dynastic histories. Its scope, however, has been limited in later times, so far as the Historiographer's Department is concerned, to such officials as have been named by Imperial edict for inclusion in the national records. Consequently, there has always been a vast output of private biographical literature, dealing with the lives of poets, painters, priests, hermits, villains, and others, whose good and evil deeds would have been long since forgotten, like those of the heroes before Agamemnon, but for the care of some enthusiastic biographer.

Among our eight or ten collections of this kind, there is one which deserves a special notice. This work is entitled *Biographies of Eminent Women,* and it fills four extra-large volumes, containing 310 lives in all. The idea of thus immortalising the most deserving of his countrywomen first occurred to a writer named Liu Hsiang, who flourished just before the

Christian era. I am not aware that his original work is still procurable; the present work was based upon one by another writer, of the third century A.D., and is brought down to modern times, being published in 1779. Each biography is accompanied by a full-page illustration of some scene in which the lady distinguished herself,—all from the pencil of a well-known artist.

Three good-sized encyclopædias, uniformly bound up in ninety-eight large volumes, may fairly claim a moment's notice, not only as evidencing the persistent literary industry of the Chinese, but because they are all three perfect mines of information on subjects of interest to the foreign student.

The first dates from the very beginning of the ninth century, and deals chiefly with the Administration of Government, Political Economy, and National Defences, besides Rites, Music, and subordinate questions.

The second dates from the twelfth century, and deals with the same subjects, having additional sections on History and Chronology, Writing, Pronunciation, Astronomy, Bibliography, Prodigies, Fauna and Flora, Foreign Nations, etc.

The third, and best known to foreign scholars, is the encyclopædia of Ma Tuan-lin of the fourteenth century. It is on much the same lines as the other two, being actually based upon the first, but has of course the advantage of being some centuries later.

The above three works are in a uniform edition, published in the middle of the eighteenth century under orders from the Emperor Ch'ien Lung.

There are also several other encyclopædias of information on general topics, extending to a good many volumes in each case.

One of these contains interesting extracts on all manner of subjects taken from the lighter literature of China, such as Dreams, Palmistry, Reminiscences of a Previous State of Existence, and even Resurrection after Death. It was cut on blocks for printing in A.D. 981, only fifty years after the first edition of the Confucian Canon was printed. The Cambridge copy cannot claim to date from 981, but it does date from 1566.

Another work of the same kind was the *San Ts'ai T'u Hui*, issued in 1609, which is bound up in seventeen thick volumes. It is especially interesting for the variety of topics on which information is given, and also because it is profusely illustrated with full-page woodcuts. It has chapters on Geography, with maps; on Ethnology, Language, the Arts and Sciences, and even on various forms of Athletics, including the feats of rope-dancers and acrobats, sword-play, boxing, wrestling, and foot-ball.

Under Tricks and Magic we see a man swallowing a sword, or walking through fire, while hard by an acrobat is bending backward and drinking from cups arranged upon the ground.

The chapters on Drawing are exceptionally good; they contain some specimen landscapes of almost faultless perspective, and also clever examples of free-hand drawing. Portrait-painting is dealt with, and ten illustrations are given of the ten angles at which a face may be drawn. The first shows one-tenth of the face from the right side, the second two-tenths, and so on, waxing to full-face five-tenths; then waning sets in on the left side, four, three, and two-tenths, until ten-tenths shows nothing more than the back of the sitter's head.

There is a well-known Chinese story which tells how a very stingy man took a paltry sum of money to an artist—payment is always exacted in advance—and asked him to paint his portrait. The artist at once complied with his request, but in an hour or so, when the portrait was finished, nothing was visible save the back of the sitter's head. "What does this mean?" cried the latter, indignantly. "Oh," replied the artist, "I thought a man who paid so little as you wouldn't care to show his face!"

---

Perhaps some one may wonder how it is possible to arrange an encyclopædia for reference when the language in which it is written happens to possess no alphabet.

Arrangement under Categories is the favourite method, and it is employed in the following way:—

A number of such words as Heaven, Earth, Time, Man, Plants, Beasts, Birds, Fishes, Minerals, and others are chosen, and the subjects are grouped under these headings. Thus, Eclipses would come under Heaven, Geomancy under Earth, the Passions under Man, though all classification is not quite so simple as these specimens, and search is often prolonged by failing to hit upon the right Category. Even when the Category is the right one, many pages of Index have frequently to be turned over; but once fix the reference in the Index, and the rest is easy, the catch-word in each case being printed on the margin of each page, just where the finger comes when turning the pages rapidly over.

The Chinese are very fond of collections of reprints, published in uniform editions and often extending to several hundred volumes. My earliest acquaintance with literature is associated with such a collection in English. It was called *The Family Library*, and ran to over a hundred volumes, if I recollect rightly, and included the works of Washington Irving and the immortal story of *Rip Van Winkle*. There is also a Chinese Rip Van Winkle, a tale of a man who, wandering one day in the mountains, came upon two boys playing checkers; and after watching them for some time, and eating some dates they gave him, he discovered that the handle of an axe he was carrying had mouldered into dust. Returning home, he found, as the Chinese poet puts it,

"City and suburb as of old,
 But hearts that loved him long since cold."

Seven generations had passed away in the interim.

The Cambridge Library possesses several of these collections of reprints. One of them is perhaps extra valuable because the wooden blocks from which it was printed were destroyed during the T'ai-p'ing Rebellion, some forty years ago.

I may mention here, though not properly belonging to this section, that we possess a good collection of the curious pamphlets issued by the T'ai-p'ing rebels.

Other interesting works to be found in Division B are the Statutes of the present dynasty, which began in 1644, and even those of the previous dynasty, the latter being an edition of 1576.

Then there is the Penal Code of this dynasty, in several editions; various collections of precedents; handbooks for magistrates, with recorded decisions and illustrative cases.

A magistrate or judge in China is not expected to know anything about law.

Attached to the office of every official who may be called upon to try criminal cases is a law expert, to whom the judge or magistrate may refer, when he has any doubt, in private, just as our unpaid justices of the peace in England refer for guidance to the qualified official attached to the court.

Before passing on to the next section, one last volume, taken at haphazard, bears the weird title, *A Record in Dark Blood.* This work contains notices of eminent statesmen and others, who met violent deaths, each accompanied by a telling illustration of the tragic scene. Some of the incidents go far to dispose of the belief that patriotism is quite unknown to the Chinese.

---

Division C is devoted to Geography and to Topography. Here stands the Imperial Geography of the Empire, in twenty-four large volumes, with maps, in the edition of 1745. Here, too, stand many of the Topographies for which China is justly celebrated. Every Prefecture and every District, or Department,—and the latter number about fifteen hundred,—has its Topography, a kind of local history, with all the noticeable features of the District, its bridges, temples, and like buildings, duly described, together with biographies of all natives of the District who have risen to distinction in any way. Each Topography would occupy about two feet of shelf; consequently a complete collection of all the Topographies of China, piled one upon the other, would form a vertical column as high as the Eiffel Tower. Yet Topography is only an outlying branch of Chinese literature.

Division C further contains the oldest printed book in the Cambridge University Library, and a very interesting one to boot. It is entitled *An Account of Strange Nations,* and was published between 1368 and 1398. Its contents consist of short notices of about 150 nationalities known more or less to the Chinese, and the value of these is much enhanced by the woodcuts which accompany each notice.

Among the rest we find Koreans, Japanese, Hsiung-nu (the forefathers of the Huns), Kitan Tartars, tribes of Central Asia, Arabs, Persians, and even Portuguese, Jean de Montecorvino, who had been appointed archbishop of Peking in 1308, having died there in 1330. Of course there are a few pictures of legendary peoples, such as the Long-armed Nation, the One-eyed Nation, the Dog-headed Nation, the Anthropophagi,

"and men whose heads
Do grow beneath their shoulders."

There is also an account of Fusang, the country where grew the famous plant which some have tried to identify with the Mexican aloe, thus securing the discovery of America for the Chinese.

The existence of many of these nations is duly recorded by Pliny in his *Natural History,* in words curiously identical with those we find in the Chinese records.

Some strange birds and animals are given at the end of this book, the most interesting of all being an accurate picture of the zebra, here called the *Fu-lu,* which means "Deer of Happiness," but which is undoubtedly a rough attempt at *fara,* an old Arabic term for the wild ass. Now, the zebra being quite unknown in Asia, the puzzle is, how the Chinese came to be so well acquainted with it at that early date.

The condition of the book is as good as could be expected, after six hundred years of wear and tear. Each leaf, here and there defective, is carefully mounted on sheets of stiff paper, and all together very few characters are really illegible, though sometimes the paper has slipped upon the printing-block, and has thus given, in several cases, a double outline.

Alongside of this stands the modern work of the kind, published in 1761, with an introductory poem from the pen of the Emperor Ch'ien Lung. It contains a much longer list of nations, including the British, French, Spanish, Dutch, Russians, Swedes, and others, and the illustrations—a man and woman of each country—are perfect triumphs of the block-cutter's art, the lines being inconceivably fine.

---

Division D contains Poetry, Novels, and Plays. Under Poetry, in addition to collections of the works of this or that writer, there are numerous anthologies, to which the Chinese are very partial. The mass of Chinese poetry is so vast, that it is hopeless for the general reader to do much more than familiarise himself with the best specimens of the greatest poets. It is interesting to note that all the more extensive anthologies include a considerable number of poems by women, some of quite a high order.

Two years ago, an eminent scientist at Cambridge said to me, "Have the Chinese anything in the nature of poetry in their language?" In reply to this, I told him of a question once put to me by a friendly Mandarin in China: "Have you foreigners got books in your honourable country?" We are apt to smile at Chinese ignorance of Western institutions; but if we were Chinamen, the smile perhaps would sometimes be the other way about.

Such novels as we have in our library belong entirely to what may be called the classical school, and may from many points of view be regarded as genuine works of art. Besides these, there is in the market a huge quantity of fiction which appeals to the less highly educated classes, and even to those who are absolutely unable to read. For the latter, there are professional readers and story-tellers, who may often be seen at some convenient point in a Chinese town, delighting large audiences of coolies with tales of love, and war, and heroism, and self-sacrifice. These readers do not read the actual words of the book, which no coolie would understand, but transpose the book-language into the colloquial as they go along.

*À propos* of novels, I should like just to mention one, a romantic novel of war and adventure, based upon the *History of the Three Kingdoms,* third century A.D., an epoch when China was split up under three separate sovereigns, who fought one another very much after the style of the Wars of the Roses in English history. This novel, a very long one, occupies perhaps the warmest corner in the hearts of the Chinese people. They never tire of listening to its stirring episodes, its hair-breadth escapes, its successful ruses, and its appalling combats.

Some twelve years ago, a friend of mine undertook to translate it into English. After writing out a complete translation,—a gigantic task,—he rewrote the whole from beginning to end, revising every page thoroughly. In the spring of 1900, after ten years of toil, it was ready for the press; three months later it had been reduced to ashes by the Boxers at Peking.

"Sunt lacrymae rerum ..."

Chinese plays in the acting editions may be bought singly at street-stalls for less than a cent apiece. For the library, many good collections have been made, and published in handsome editions.

This class of literature, however, does not stand upon a high level, but corresponds with the low social status of the actor; and it is a curious fact—true also of novels—that many of the best efforts are anonymous.

Plays by women are also to be found; but I have never yet come across, either on the stage or in literature, any of those remarkable dramas which are supposed to run on month after month, even into years.

---

Division E is a very important one for students of the Chinese language. Here we find a number of works of reference, most of which may be characterised as indispensable, and the great majority of which are easily procurable at the present day.

Beginning with dictionaries, we have the famous work of Hsü Shên, who died about A.D. 120. There was at that date no such thing as a Chinese dictionary, although the language had already been for some centuries ripe for such a production, and accordingly Hsü Shên set to work to fill the void. He collected 9353 written characters,—presumably all that were in existence at the time,—to which he added 1163 duplicates, *i.e.* various forms of writing the same character, and then arranged them in groups under those parts which, as we have already seen in the preceding Lecture, are indicators of the direction in which the sense of a character is to be looked for. Thus, all characters containing the element 犭 "dog" were brought together; all those containing 艹 "vegetation," 疒 "disease," etc.

So far as we know, this system originated with him; and we are therefore not surprised to find that in his hands it was on a clumsier scale than that in vogue to-day. Hsü Shên uses no fewer than 540 of these indicators, and even when the indicator to a character is satisfactorily ascertained, it still remains to search through all the characters under that particular group. Printing from movable types would have been impossible under such a system.

In the modern standard dictionary, published in 1716, under the direction of the Emperor K'ang Hsi, there are only 214 indicators employed, and there is a further sub-arrangement of these groups according to the number of strokes in the other, the phonetic portion of the character. Thus, the indicators "hand," "wood," "fire," "water," or whatever it may be, settle the group in which a given character will be found, and the number of strokes in the remaining portion will refer it to a comparatively small sub-group, from which it can be readily picked out. For instance, 松 "a fir tree" will be found under the indicator 木 "tree," sub-group No. 4, because the remaining portion 公 consists of four strokes in writing.

Good copies of this dictionary are not too easily obtained nowadays. The "Palace" edition, as it is called, is on beautifully white paper, and is a splendid specimen of typography.

A most wonderful literary feat was achieved under the direction of the before-mentioned Emperor K'ang Hsi, when a general Concordance to the phraseology of all literature was compiled and published for general use. Word-concordances to the Bible and to Shakespeare are generally looked upon as no small undertakings, but what about a phrase-concordance to all literature? Well, in 1711 this was successfully carried out, and remains to-day as a monument of the literary enterprise of the great Manchu-Tartar monarch with whose name it is inseparably associated.

The term "literature" here means serious literature, the classics, histories, poetry, and the works of philosophers, of recognised authorities, and of brilliant writers generally.

It was not possible, for obvious reasons, to arrange this collection of phrases according to the 214 indicators, as in a dictionary of words. It is arranged according to the Tones and Rhymes.

Let me try to express all this in terms of English literature. Reading a famous poem, I come across the lines

"And every shepherd tells his tale
Under the hawthorn in the dale."

Now suppose that I do not know the meaning of "tells his tale." [I recollect perfectly that as a boy I thought it meant "whispered the old story into the ear of a shepherdess."] I determine to hunt it up in the Concordance. First of all, I find out from the Dictionary, if I do not know, to what Tone *tale*, always the last word of the phrase, belongs. Under that tone will be found various groups of words, each with a key-word which is called the Rhyme, that is to say, a key-word with which all the words in this group rhyme. There are only 106 of these key-words all together distributed over the Tones, and every word in the Chinese language must rhyme with one of them.

The question of rhyme in Chinese is a curious one, and before going any farther it may be as well to try to clear it up a little. All Chinese poetry is in rhyme; there is no such thing as blank verse. The *Odes*, collected and edited by Confucius, provide the standard of rhyme. Any words which are found to rhyme there may be used as rhymes anywhere else, and no others. The result is, that the number of rhyme-groups is restricted to 106; and not only that, but of course words which rhymed to the ear five hundred years B.C. do so no longer in 1902. Yet such are the only authorised rhymes to be used in poetry, and any attempt to ignore the rule would insure disastrous failure at the public examinations.

This point may to some extent be illustrated in English. The first two lines of the *Canterbury Tales*, which I will take to represent the *Odes*, run thus in modern speech:—

"When that Aprilis with his showers sweet,
The drought of March hath pierced to the root."

No one nowadays rhymes *sweet* with *root*. Neither did Chaucer; the two words, *sote* and *rote*, were in his days perfect rhymes. But if we were Chinese, we should now rhyme *sweet* with *root*, because, so to speak, Chaucer did so.

When the Tone of a word is known, it is also known in which quarter of the whole work to look; and when the Rhyme is known, it is also known in which part of that quarter the key-word, or rhyme, will be found. Suppose the key-word to be *gale*, it might be necessary to turn over a good many pages before finding, neatly printed in the margin, the required word, *tale*. Under *tale* I should first of all find phrases of two words, *e.g.* "traveller's tale," "fairy-tale"; and I should have to look on until I came to groups of three characters, *e.g.* "old wife's tale," "tells his tale," and so forth. Finally, under "tells his tale" I should still not find, what all students would like so much, a plain explanation of what the phrase means, but only a collection of the chief passages in literature in which "tells his tale" occurs. In one of these there would probably be some allusion to sheep, and in another to counting, and so it would become pretty plain that when a shepherd "tells his tale," he does not whisper soft nothings into the ear of a shepherdess, but is much more prosaically engaged in counting the number of his sheep.

Our Cambridge copy of the Concordance is bound up in 44 thick volumes. Each volume contains on an average 840 pages, and each page about 400 characters. This gives a sum total of about 37,000 pages, and about 15,000,000 characters. Translated into English, this work would be one-third as large again, 100 pages of Chinese text being equal to about 130 of English.

In the year 1772 the enlightened Emperor Ch'ien Lung, who then sat upon the throne, gave orders that a descriptive Catalogue should be prepared of the books in the Imperial Library. And in order to enhance its literary value, his Majesty issued invitations to the leading provincial officials to take part in the enterprise by securing and forwarding to Peking any rare books they might be able to come across.

The scheme proved in every way successful. Many old works were rescued from oblivion and ultimate destruction, and in 1795 a very wonderful Catalogue was laid before the world in print. It fills twenty-six octavo volumes of about five hundred pages to each, the works enumerated being divided into four classes,—the Confucian Canon, History, Philosophy, and General Literature. Under each work we have first of all an historical sketch of its origin, with date of publication, etc., when known; and secondly, a careful critique dealing with its merits and defects. All together, some eight thousand to ten thousand works are entered and examined as above, and the names of those officials who responded to the Imperial call are always scrupulously recorded in connection with the books they supplied.

Among many illustrated books, there is a curious volume in the Library published about twenty-five years ago, which contains short notices of all the Senior Classics of the Ming dynasty, A.D. 1368-1644. They number only seventy-six in all, because the triennial examination had not then come into force; whereas during the present dynasty, between 1644 and twenty-five years ago, a shorter period, there have been no fewer than one hundred Senior Classics, whose names are all duly recorded in a Supplement.

The pictures which accompany the letterpress are sometimes of quite pathetic interest.

In one instance, the candidate, after his journey to Peking, where the examination is held, has gone home to await the result, and is sitting at dinner with his friends, when suddenly the much-longed-for messenger bursts in with the astounding news. In the old days this news was carried to all parts of the country by trained runners; nowadays the telegraph wires do the business at a great saving of time and muscle, with the usual sacrifice of romance.

Another student has gone home, and settled down to work again, not daring even to hope for success; but overcome with fatigue and anxiety, he falls asleep over his books. In the accompanying picture we see his dream, —a thin curl, as it were of vapour, coming forth from the top of his head and broadening out as it goes, until wide enough to contain the representation of a man, in feature like himself, surrounded by an admiring crowd, who acclaim him Senior Classic. With a start the illusion is dispelled, and the dreamer awakes to find himself famous.

To those who have followed me so far, it must, I hope, be clear that, whatever else the Chinese may be, they are above all a literary people. They have cultivated literature as no other people ever has done, and they cultivate it still.

Literary merit leads to an official career, the only career worth anything in the eyes of the Chinese nation.

From his earliest school days the Chinese boy is taught that men without education are but horses or cows in coats and trousers, and that success at the public examinations is the greatest prize this world has to offer.

To be among the fortunate three hundred out of about twelve thousand candidates, who contend once every three years for the highest degree, is to be enrolled among the Immortals for ever; while the Senior Classic at a final competition before the Emperor not only covers himself, but even his remote ancestors, his native village, his district, his prefecture, and even his province, with a glory almost of celestial splendour.

# DEMOCRATIC CHINA

Theoretically speaking, the Empire of China is ruled by an autocratic monarch, responsible only to God, whose representative he is on earth.

Once every year the Emperor prays at the Temple of Heaven, and sacrifices in solemn state upon its altar. He puts himself, as it were, into communication with the Supreme Being, and reports upon the fidelity with which he has carried out his Imperial trust.

If the Emperor rules wisely and well, with only the happiness of his people at heart, there will be no sign from above, beyond peace and plenty in the Empire, and now and then a double ear of corn in the fields—a phenomenon which will be duly recorded in the *Peking Gazette*. But should there be anything like laxness or incapacity, or still worse, degradation and vice, then a comet may perhaps appear, a pestilence may rage, or a famine, to warn the erring ruler to give up his evil ways.

And just as the Emperor is responsible to Heaven, so are the viceroys and governors of the eighteen provinces—to speak only of China proper—nominally responsible to him, in reality to the six departments of state at Peking, which constitute the central government, and to which a seventh has recently been added—a department for foreign affairs.

So long as all goes well—and in ordinary times that "all" is confined to a regular and sufficient supply of revenue paid into the Imperial Treasury—viceroys and governors of provinces are, as nearly as can be, independent rulers, each in his own domain.

For purposes of government, in the ordinary sense of the term, the 18 provinces are subdivided into 80 areas known as "circuits," and over each of these is set a high official, who is called an intendant of circuit, or in Chinese a *Tao-t'ai*. His circuit consists of 2 or more prefectures, of which there are in all 282 distributed among the 80 circuits, or about an average of 3 prefectures to each.

Every prefecture is in turn subdivided into several magistracies, of which there are 1477 in all, distributed among the 282 prefectures, or about an average of 5 magistracies to each.

Immediately below the magistrates may be said to come the people; though naturally an official who rules over an area as big as an average English county can scarcely be brought into personal touch with all those under his jurisdiction. This difficulty is bridged over by the appointment of a number of head men, or headboroughs, who are furnished with wooden seals, and who are held responsible for the peace and good order of the wards or boroughs over which they are set. The post is considered an honourable one, involving as it does a quasi-official status. It is also more or less lucrative, as it is necessary that all petitions to the magistrate, all conveyances of land, and other legal instruments, should bear the seal of the head man, as a guarantee of good faith, a small fee being payable on each notarial act.

On the other hand, the post is occasionally burdensome and trying in the extreme. For instance, if a head man fails to produce any criminals or accused persons, either belonging to, or known to be, in his district, he is liable to be bambooed or otherwise severely punished.

In ordinary life the head man is not distinguishable from the masses of his fellow-countrymen. He may often be seen working like the rest, and even walking about with bare legs and bare feet.

Thus in a descending scale we have the Emperor, the viceroys and governors of the 18 provinces, the intendants, or *Tao-t'ais*, of the 80 circuits, the prefects of the 282 prefectures, the magistrates of the 1477 magistracies, the myriad headboroughs, and the people.

The district magistrates, so far as officials are concerned, are the real rulers of China, and in conjunction with the prefects are popularly called "father-and-mother" officials, as though they stood *in loco parentium* to the people, whom, by the way, they in turn often speak of, even in official documents, as "the babies."

The ranks of these magistrates are replenished by drafts of those *literati* who have succeeded in taking the third, or highest, degree. Thus, the first step on the ladder is open to all who can win their way by successful competition at certain literary examinations, so long as each candidate can show that none of his ancestors for three generations have been either actors, barbers and chiropodists, priests, executioners, or official servants.

Want of means may be said to offer no obstacle in China to ambition and desire for advancement. The slightest aptitude in a boy for learning would be carefully noted, and if found to be the genuine article, would be still more carefully fostered. Not only are there plenty of free schools in China, but there are plenty of persons ready to help in so good a cause. Many a high official has risen from the furrowed fields, his educational expenses as a student, and his travelling expenses as a candidate, being paid by subscription in his native place. Once successful, he can easily find a professional money-lender who will provide the comparatively large sums required for his outfit and journey to his post, whither this worthy actually accompanies him, to remain until he is repaid in full, with interest.

A successful candidate, however, is not usually sent straight from the examination-hall to occupy the important position of district magistrate. He is attached to some magistracy as an expectant official, and from time to time his capacity is tested by a case, more or less important, which is entrusted to his management as deputy.

The duties of a district magistrate are so numerous and so varied that one man could not possibly cope with them all. At the same time he is fully responsible. In addition to presiding over a court of first instance for all criminal trials in his district, he has to act as coroner (without a jury) at all inquests, collect and remit the land-tax, register all conveyances of land and house-property, act as preliminary examiner of candidates for literary degrees, and perform a host of miscellaneous offices, even to praying for rain or fine weather in cases of drought or inundation. He is up, if anything, before the lark; and at night, often late at night, he is listening to the protestations of prisoners or bambooing recalcitrant witnesses.

But inasmuch as the district may often be a large one, and two inquests may be going on in two different directions on the same day, or there may be other conflicting claims upon his time, he has constantly to depute his duties to a subordinate, whose usual duties, if he has any, have to be taken by some one else, and so on. Thus it is that the expectant official every now and then gets his chance.

This scheme leaves out of consideration a number of provincial officials, who preside over departments which branch, as it were, from the main trunk, and of whom a few words only need now be said.

There are several "commissioners," as they are sometimes called; for instance, the commissioner of finance, otherwise known as the provincial treasurer, who is charged with the fiscal administration of his particular province, and who controls the nomination of nearly all the minor appointments in the civil service, subject to the approval of the governor.

Then there is the commissioner of justice, or provincial judge, responsible for the due administration of justice in his province.

There is also the salt commissioner, who collects the revenue derived from the government monopoly of the salt trade; and the grain commissioner, who looks after the grain-tax, and sees that the tribute rice is annually forwarded to Peking, for the use of the Imperial Court.

There are also military officials, belonging to two separate and distinct army organisations.

The Manchus, when they conquered the Empire, placed garrisons of their own troops, under the command of Manchu generals, at various important strategic points; and the Tartar generals, as they are called, still remain, ranking nominally just above the viceroy of the province, over whose actions they are supposed to keep a careful watch.

Then there is a provincial army, with a provincial commander-in-chief, etc.

Now let us return to the main trunk, working upward by way of recapitulation.

We have reached the people and their head men, or headboroughs, over whom is set the magistrate, with a nominal salary which would be quite insufficient for his needs, even if he were ever to draw it. For he has a large staff to keep up; some few of whom, no doubt, keep themselves by fees and *douceurs* of various kinds obtained from litigants and others who have business to transact.

The income on which the magistrate lives, and from which, after a life of incessant toil, he saves a moderate competence for the requirements of his family, is deducted from the gross revenues of his magistracy, leaving a net amount to be forwarded to the Imperial Treasury. So long as his superiors are satisfied with what he remits, no questions are asked as to original totals. It is recognised that he must live, and the value of every magistracy is known within a few hundred ounces of silver one way or the other.

Above the magistrate, and in control of several magistracies, comes the prefect, who has to satisfy his superiors in the same way. He has the general supervision of all civil business in his prefecture, and to him must be referred every appeal case from the magistracies under his jurisdiction, before it can be filed in a higher court.

Above him comes the intendant of circuit, or *Tao-t'ai*, in control of several prefectures, to whom the same rule applies as to satisfying demands of superiors; and above him come the governor and viceroy, who must also satisfy the demands of the state departments in Peking.

It would now appear, from what has been already stated, that all a viceroy or governor has to do is to exact sufficient revenue from immediate subordinates, and leave them to exact the amounts necessary from *their* subordinates, and so on down the scale until we reach the people. The whole question therefore resolves itself into this, What can the people be made to pay?

The answer to that question will be somewhat of a staggerer to those who from distance, or from want of close observation, regard the Chinese as a down-trodden people, on a level with the Fellahin of Egypt in past times. For the answer, so far as my own experience goes, is that only so much can be got out of the Chinese people as the people themselves are ready and willing to pay. In other words, with all their show of an autocratic ruler and a paternal government, the people of China tax themselves.

I am now about to do more than state this opinion; I am going to try to prove it.

The philosopher Mencius, who flourished about one hundred years after Confucius, and who is mainly responsible for the final triumph of the Confucian doctrine, was himself not so much a teacher of ethics as a teacher of political science. He spent a great part of his life wandering from feudal state to feudal state, advising the various vassal nobles how to order their dominions with the maximum of peace and prosperity and the minimum of misery and bloodshed.

One of these nobles, Duke Wên, asked Mencius concerning the proper way to govern a state.

"The affairs of the people," replied the philosopher, "must not be neglected. For the way of the people is thus: If they have a fixed livelihood, their hearts will also be fixed; but if they have not a fixed livelihood, neither will their hearts be fixed. And if they have not fixed hearts, there is nothing in the way of crime which they will not commit. Then, when they have involved themselves in guilt, to follow up and punish them,—this is but to ensnare them."

In another passage Mencius says: "The tyrants of the last two dynasties, Chieh and Chou, lost the Empire because they lost the people, by which I mean that they lost the hearts of the people. There is a way to get the Empire;—get the people, and you have the Empire. There is a way to get the people;—get their hearts, and you have them. There is a way to get their hearts;—do for them what they wish, and avoid doing what they do not wish."

Those are strong words, especially when we consider that they come from one of China's most sacred books, regarded by the Chinese with as much veneration as the Bible by us,—a portion of that Confucian Canon, the principles of which it is the object of every student to master, and should be the object of every Chinese official to carry into practice.

But those words are mild compared with another utterance by Mencius in the same direction.

"The people are the most important element in a nation; the gods come next; the sovereign is the least important of all."

We have here, in Chinese dress, wherein indeed much of Western wisdom will be found, if students will only look for it, very much the same sentiment as in the familiar lines by Oliver Goldsmith:—

"Princes and lords may flourish or may fade,—
A breath can make them, as a breath has made;
But a bold peasantry, their country's pride
When once destroyed, can never be supplied."

The question now arises, Are all these solemn sayings of Mencius to be regarded as nothing more than mere literary rodomontade, wherewith to beguile an enslaved people? Do the mandarins keep the word of promise to the ear and break it to the hope? Or do the Chinese people enjoy in real life the recognition which should be accorded to them by the terms of the Confucian Canon?

Every one who has lived in China, and has kept his eyes open, must have noticed what a large measure of personal freedom is enjoyed by even the meanest subject of the Son of Heaven. Any Chinaman may travel all over China without asking any one's leave to start, and without having to report himself, or be reported by his innkeeper, at any place at which he may choose to stop. He requires no passport. He may set up any legitimate business at any place. He is not even obliged to be educated, or to follow any particular calling. He is not obliged to serve as a soldier or sailor. There are no sumptuary laws, nor even any municipal laws. Outside the penal code, which has been pronounced by competent Western lawyers to be a very ably constructed instrument of government, there is nothing at all in the way of law, civil law being altogether absent as a state institution. Even the penal code is not too rigidly enforced. So long as a man keeps clear of secret societies and remains a decent and respectable member of his family and of his clan, he has very little to fear from the officials. The old ballad of the husbandman, which has come down to us from a very early date indeed, already hints at some such satisfactory state of things. It runs thus:—

"Work, work,—from the rising sun
Till sunset comes and the day is done
I plough the sod,
And harrow the clod,
And meat and drink both come to me,—
Ah, what care I for the powers that be?"

Many petty offences which are often dealt with very harshly in England, pass in China almost unnoticed. No shopkeeper or farmer would be fool enough to charge a hungry man with stealing food, for the simple reason that no magistrate would convict. It is the shopkeeper's or farmer's business to see that such petty thefts cannot occur. Various other points might be noticed; but we must get back to taxation, which is really the *crux* of the whole position.

All together the Chinese people may be said to be lightly taxed. There is the land-tax, in money and in kind; a tax on salt; and various *octroi* and customs-duties, all of which are more or less fixed quantities, so that the approximate amount which each province should contribute to the central government is well known at Peking, just as it is well known in each province what amounts, approximately speaking, should be handed up by the various grades of territorial officials.

I have already stated that municipal government is unknown; consequently there are no municipal rates to be paid, no water-rate, no poor-rate, and not a cent for either sanitation or education. And so long as the Imperial taxes are such as the people have grown accustomed to, they are paid cheerfully, even if sometimes with difficulty, and nothing is said.

A curious instance of this conservative spirit in the Chinese people, even when operating against their own interests, may be found in the tax known as *likin*, against which foreign governments have struggled so long in vain. This tax, originally one-tenth per cent on all sales, was voluntarily imposed upon themselves by the people, among whom it was at first very popular, with a view of making up the deficiency in the land-tax of China caused by the T'ai-p'ing Rebellion and subsequent troubles. It was to be set apart for military purposes only,—hence its common name "war-tax,"—and was alleged by the Tsung-li Yamên to be adopted merely as a temporary measure. Yet, though forty years have elapsed, it still continues to be collected as if it were one of the fundamental taxes of the Empire, and the objections to it are raised, not by the people of China, but by foreign merchants with whose trade it interferes.

Here we have already one instance of voluntary self-taxation on the part of the people; what I have yet to show is that all taxation, even though not initiated as in this case by the people, must still receive the stamp of popular approval before being put into force. On this point I took a good many notes during a fairly long residence in China, leading to conclusions which seem to me irresistible.

Let us suppose that the high authorities of a province have determined, for pressing reasons, to make certain changes in the incidence of taxation, or have called upon their subordinates to devise means for causing larger sums to find their way into the provincial treasury. The invariable usage, previous to the imposition of a new tax, or change in the old, is for the magistrate concerned to send for the leading merchants whose interests may be involved, or for the headboroughs and village elders, according to the circumstances in each case, and to discuss the proposition in private. Over an informal entertainment, over tea and pipes, the magistrate pleads the necessities of the case, and the peremptory orders of his superiors; the merchants or village elders, feeling that, as in the case of *likin* above mentioned, when taxes come they come to stay, resist on principle the new departure by every argument at their control. The negotiation ends, in ninety-nine instances out of a hundred, in a compromise. In the hundredth instance the people may think it right to give way, or the mandarin may give way, in which case things remain *in statu quo*, and nothing further is heard of the matter.

There occur cases, however, happily rare, in which neither will give way—at first. Then comes the tug of war. A proclamation is issued, describing the tax, or the change, or whatever it may be, and the people, if their interests are sufficiently involved, prepare to resist.

Combination has been raised in China to the level of a fine art. Nowhere on earth can be found such perfect cohesion of units against forces which would crush each unit, taken individually, beyond recognition. Every trade, every calling, even the meanest, has its guild, or association, the members of which are ever ready to protect one another with perfect unanimity, and often great self-sacrifice. And combination is the weapon with which the people resist, and successfully resist, any attempt on the part of the governing classes to lay upon them loads greater than they can or will bear. The Chinese are withal an exceptionally law-abiding people, and entertain a deep-seated respect for authority. But their obedience and their deference have pecuniary limits.

I will now pass from the abstract to the concrete, and draw upon my note-book for illustrations of this theory that the Chinese are a self-taxing and self-governing people.

Under date October 10, 1880, from Chung-king in the province of Ssŭch'uan, the following story will be found in the *North China Herald*, told by a correspondent:—

"Yesterday the Pah-shien magistrate issued a proclamation, saying that he was going to raise a tax of 200 *cash* on each pig killed by the pork-butchers of this city, and the butchers were to reimburse themselves by adding 2 *cash* per *pound* to the price of pork. The butchers, who had already refused to pay 100 *cash* per hog, under the late magistrate, were not likely to submit to the payment of 200 under this one, and so resolved not to kill pigs until the grievance was removed; and this morning a party of them went about the town and seized all the pork they saw exposed for sale. Then the whole of the butchers, over five hundred at least, shut themselves up in their guild, where the magistrate tried to force an entry with two hundred or three hundred of his runners. The butchers, however, refused to open the door, and the magistrate had to retire very much excited, threatening to bring them to terms. People are inclined to think the magistrate acted wrongly in taking a large force with him, saying he ought to have gone alone."

Three days later, October 13:—

"There is great excitement throughout the city, and I am told that the troops are under arms. I have heard several volleys of small arms being fired off, as if in platoon exercise. All the shops are shut, people being afraid that the authorities may deal severely with the butchers, and that bad characters will profit by the excitement to rob and plunder the shops."

Two days later, October 15:—

"The pork-butchers are still holding out in their guild-house, and refuse to recommence business until the officials have promised that the tax on pigs will not be enforced now or hereafter. The prefect has been going the rounds of the city calling on the good people of his prefecture to open their shops and transact business as usual, saying that the tax on pigs did not concern other people, but only the butchers."

One day later, October 16:—

"The Pah-shien magistrate has issued a proclamation apologising to the people generally, and to the butchers particularly, for his share of the work in trying to increase the obnoxious tax on pigs. So the officials have all miserably failed in squeezing a *cash* out of the 'sovereign people' of Ssŭch'uan."

I have a similar story from Hangchow, in Chehkiang, under date April 10, 1889, which begins as follows:—

"The great city of Hangchow is extremely dry. There are probably seven hundred thousand people here, but not a drop of tea can be bought in any of the public tea-houses. There is a strike in tea. The tea-houses are all closed by common agreement, to resist a tax, imposed in the beginning of the year, to raise money for the sufferers by famine."

In the next communication from this correspondent, we read, "The strike of the keepers of tea-shops ended very quietly a few days after it began, by the officials agreeing to accept the sum of fifteen hundred dollars once for all, and release tea from taxation."

This is what happened recently in Pakhoi, in the province of Kuangtung: —

"Without the consent of the dealers, a new local tax was imposed on the raw opium in preparation for use in the opium shops. The imposition of this tax brought to light the fact, hitherto kept secret, that of the opium consumed in Pakhoi and its district, only sixty-two per cent was imported drug, the remaining third being native opium, which was smuggled into Pakhoi, and avoided all taxation. The new tax brought this smuggled opium under contribution, and this was more than the local opium interest would stand. The opium dealers adopted the usual tactics of shutting their shops, thus transferring the *onus* of opposition to their customers. These last paid a threatening visit to the chief authority of Pakhoi, and then wrecked the newly established tax-office. This indication of popular feeling was enough for the local authorities at Lien-chou, the district city, and the tax was changed so as to fall on the foreign opium, the illicit native supply being discreetly ignored, and all rioters forgiven."

So much for taxation. Let us take an instance of interference with prescriptive rights, in connection with the great incorruptible viceroy, Chang Chih-tung, to whom we are all so much indebted for his attitude during the Siege of the Legations in 1900.

Ten years ago, when starting his iron-works at Wuchang, in the province of Hupeh, he ordered the substitution of a drawbridge over a creek for the old bridge which had stood there from time immemorial, the object being to let steamers pass freely up and down. Unfortunately, the old bridge was destroyed before the new one was ready. What was the result?

"The people rushed to the Yamên, and insisted by deputation and mass-brawling on the restoration of the bridge.

"Finally, the viceroy thought it worth his while to issue a rhyming proclamation, assuring the people that what he was doing was for their good, and justifying his several schemes."

Yet Chang Chih-tung always has been, and is still, one of the strongest officials who ever sat upon a viceroy's throne.

In November, 1882, there was a very serious military riot in Hankow, on the opposite side of the Yang-tsze to Wuchang. It arose out of a report that four soldiers had been arrested and were to be secretly beheaded the same night. This rising might have assumed very serious dimensions, but for the prompt submission of the viceroy to the soldiers' demands. As it was, the whole city was thrown into a state of the utmost alarm. Few of the inhabitants slept through the night. The streets were filled with a terror-stricken population, expecting at any moment to hear that the prison doors had been forced, and the criminals let loose to join the soldiers in their determination to kill the officials, plunder the treasury, and sack the city. Many citizens are said to have fled from the place; and the sudden rush upon the *cash* shops, to convert paper notes into silver, brought some of them to the verge of bankruptcy.

I have recorded, under March, 1891, a case in which several Manchus were sentenced by the magistrate of Chinkiang, at the instance of the local general, to a bambooing for rowdy behaviour. This is what followed:—

"The friends of the prisoners, to the number of about three hundred, assembled at the city temple, vowing vengeance on the magistrate and general. They proceeded to the yamên of the general, wrecked the wall and part of the premises, and put the city in an uproar. The magistrate fled with his family to the Tao-t'ai's yamên, where two hundred regular troops were sent to protect him against the fury of the Manchus, who threatened his life."

This is what happened to another magistrate in Kiangsu. He had imprisoned a tax-collector for being in arrears with his money; and the tax-collector's wife, frantic with rage, rushed to the magistracy and demanded his release. Unfortunately, she was suffering from severe asthma; and this, coupled with her anger, caused her death actually in the magistrate's court. The people then smashed and wrecked the magistracy, and pummelled and bruised the magistrate himself, who ultimately effected his escape in disguise and hid himself in a private dwelling.

Every one who has lived in China knows how dangerous are the periods when vast numbers of students congregate for the public examinations. Here is an example.

At Canton, in June, 1880, a student took back a coat he had purchased for half a dollar at a second-hand clothes shop, and wished to have it changed. The shopkeeper gave him rather an impatient answer, and thereupon the student called in a band of his brother B.A.'s to claim justice for literature. They seized a reckoning-board, or abacus, that lay on the counter, struck one of the assistants in the shop, and drew blood. The shopkeeper then beat an alarm on his gong, and summoned friends and neighbours to the rescue. Word was at once passed to bands of students in the neighbourhood, who promptly obeyed the call of a distressed comrade, and blows were delivered right and left. The shopkeepers summoned the district magistrate to the scene. Upon his arrival he ordered several of the literary ringleaders, who had been seized and bound by the shopkeepers, to be carried off and impounded. In the course of the evening he sentenced them to be beaten. A body of more than a hundred students then went to his yamên and demanded the immediate release of the prisoners. The magistrate grew nervous, yielded to their threats, and sent several of the offending students home in sedan-chairs. The magistrate then seized the assistants in the shop where the row began and sentenced them to be beaten on the mouth.

Next morning ten thousand shops were closed in the city and suburbs. The shopkeepers said they could not do business under such an administration of law. In the course of the morning a large meeting of the students was held in a college adjoining the examination hall. The district magistrate went out to confer with them. The students cracked his gong, and shattered his sedan-chair with showers of stones, and then prodded him with their fans and umbrellas, and bespattered him with dirt as his followers tried to carry him away on their shoulders. He was quite seriously hurt.

The prefect then met a large deputation of the shopkeepers in their guild-house in the course of the day, and expressed his dissatisfaction at the way in which the district magistrate had acted. A settlement was thus reached, which included fireworks for the students, and business was resumed.

---

Any individual who is aggrieved by the action, or inaction, of a Chinese official may have immediate recourse to the following method for obtaining justice, witnessed by me twice during my residence in China, and known as "crying one's wrongs."

Dressed in the grey sackcloth garb of a mourner, the injured party, accompanied by as many friends as he or she can collect together, will proceed to the public residence of the offending mandarin, and there howl and be otherwise objectionable, day and night, until some relief is given. The populace is invariably on the side of the wronged person; and if the wrong is deep, or the delay in righting it too long, there is always great risk of an outbreak, with the usual scene of house-wrecking and general violence.

It may now well be asked, how justice can ever be administered under such circumstances, which seem enough to paralyse authority in the presence of any evil-doer who can bring up his friends to the rescue.

To begin with, there is in China, certainly at all great centres, a large criminal population without friends,—men who have fallen from their high estate through inveterate gambling, indulgence in opium-smoking, or more rarely alcohol. No one raises a finger to protect these from the utmost vengeance of the law.

Then again, the Chinese, just as they tax themselves, so do they administer justice to themselves. Trade disputes, petty and great alike, are never carried into court, there being no recognised civil law in China beyond custom; they are settled by the guilds or trades-unions, as a rule to the satisfaction of all parties. Many criminal cases are equally settled out of court, and the offender is punished by agreement of the clan-elders or heads of families, and nothing is said; for compounding a felony is not a crime, but a virtue, in the eyes of the Chinese, who look on all litigation with aversion and contempt.

In the case of murder, however, and some forms of manslaughter, the ingrained conviction that a life should always be given for a life often outweighs any money value that could be offered, and the majesty of the law is upheld at any sacrifice.

It is not uncommon for an accused person to challenge his accuser to a kind of trial by ordeal, at the local temple.

Kneeling before the altar, at midnight, in the presence of a crowd of witnesses, the accused man will solemnly burn a sheet of paper, on which he has written, or caused to be written, an oath, totally denying his guilt, and calling upon the gods to strike him dead upon the spot, or his accuser, if either one is deviating in the slightest degree from the actual truth.

This is indeed a severe ordeal to a superstitious people, whatever it may seem to us. Even the mandarins avail themselves of similar devices in cases where they are unable to clear up a mystery in the ordinary way.

In a well-known case of a murder by a gang of ruffians, the magistrate, being unable to fix the guilt of the fatal blow upon any one of the gang, told them that he was going to apply to the gods. He then caused them all to be dressed in black coats, as is usual with condemned criminals, and arranged them in a dark shed, with their faces to the wall, saying that, in response to his prayers, a demon would be sent to mark the back of the guilty man. When at length the accused were brought out of the shed, one of them actually had a white mark on his back, and he at once confessed. In order to outwit the demon he had slily placed his back against the wall, which by the magistrate's secret orders had previously received a coat of whitewash.

I will conclude with a case which came under my own personal observation, and which first set me definitely on the track of democratic government in China.

In 1882 I was vice-consul at Pagoda Anchorage, a port near the famous Foochow Arsenal which was bombarded by Admiral Courbet in 1884. My house and garden were on an eminence overlooking the arsenal, which was about half a mile distant. One morning, after breakfast, the head official servant came to tell me there was trouble at the arsenal. A military mandarin, employed there as superintendent of some department, had that morning early kicked his cook, a boy of seventeen, in the stomach, and the boy, a weakly lad, had died within an hour. The boy's widowed mother was sitting by the body in the mandarin's house, and a large crowd of workmen had formed a complete ring outside, quietly awaiting the arrival and decision of the authorities.

By five o'clock in the afternoon, a deputy had arrived from the magistracy at Foochow, twelve miles distant, empowered to hold the usual inquest on behalf of the magistrate. The inquest was duly held, and the verdict was "accidental homicide."

In shorter time than it takes me to tell the story, the deputy's sedan-chair and paraphernalia of office were smashed to atoms. He himself was seized, his official hat and robe were torn to shreds, and he was bundled unceremoniously, not altogether unbruised, through the back door and through the ring of onlookers, into the paddy-fields beyond. Then the ring closed up again, and a low, threatening murmur broke out which I could plainly hear from my garden. There was no violence, no attempt to lynch the man; the crowd merely waited for justice. That crowd remained there all night, encircling the murderer, the victim, and the mother. Bulletins were brought to me every hour, and no one went to bed.

Meanwhile the news had reached the viceroy, and by half-past nine next morning the smoke of a steam-launch was seen away up the bends of the river. This time it bore the district magistrate himself, with instructions from the viceroy to hold a new inquest.

At about ten o'clock he landed, and was received with respectful silence. By eleven o'clock the murderer's head was off and the crowd had dispersed.

# CHINA AND ANCIENT GREECE

The study of Chinese presents at least one advantage over the study of the Greek and Roman classics; I might add, of Hebrew, of Syriac, and even of Sanskrit. It may be pursued for two distinct objects. The first, and most important object to many, is to acquire a practical acquaintance with a *living* language, spoken and written by about one-third of the existing population of the earth, with a view to the extension of commercial enterprise, and to the profits and benefits which may legitimately accrue therefrom. The second is precisely that object in pursuit of which we apply ourselves so steadily to the literatures and civilisations of Greece and Rome.

Sir Richard Jebb, in his essay on "Humanism in Education," points out that even less than a hundred years ago the classics still held a virtual monopoly, so far as literary studies were concerned, in the public schools and universities of England. "The culture which they supplied," he argues, "while limited in the sphere of its operation, had long been an efficient and vital influence, not only in forming men of letters and learning, but in training men who afterwards gained distinction in public life and in various active careers."

Long centuries had fixed so firmly in the minds of our forefathers a belief, and no doubt to some extent a justifiable belief, in the perfect character of the languages, the literatures, the arts, and some of the social and political institutions of ancient Greece and Rome, that a century or so ago there seemed to be nothing else worth the attention of an intellectual man. The comparatively recent introduction of Sanskrit was received in the classical world, not merely with coldness, but with strenuous opposition; and all the genius of its pioneer scholars was needed to secure the meed of recognition which it now enjoys as an important field of research. The Regius Professorship of Greek in the University of Cambridge, England, was founded in 1540; but it was not until 1867, more than three centuries later, that Sanskrit was admitted into the university curriculum. It is still impossible to gain a degree through the medium of Chinese, but signs are not wanting that the necessity for such a step will be more widely recognised in the near future.

All the material lies ready to hand. There is a written language, which for difficulty is unrivalled, polished and perfected by centuries of the minutest scholarship, until it is impossible to conceive anything more subtly artistic as a vehicle of human thought. Those mental gymnastics, of such importance in the training of youth, which were once claimed exclusively for the languages of Greece and Rome, may be performed equally well in the Chinese language. The educated classes in China would be recognised anywhere as men of trained minds, able to carry on sustained and complex arguments without violating any of the Aristotelian canons, although as a matter of fact they never heard of Aristotle and possess no such work in all their extensive literature as a treatise on logic. The affairs of their huge empire are carried on, and in my opinion very successfully carried on—with some reservations, of course—by men who have had to get their mental gymnastics wholly and solely out of Chinese.

I am not aware that their diplomatists suffer by comparison with ours. The Marquis Tsêng and Li Hung-chang, for instance, representing opposite schools, were admitted masters of their craft, and made not a few of our own diplomatists look rather small beside them.

Speaking further of the study of the Greek and Roman classics, Sir Richard Jebb says: "There can be no better proof that such a discipline has penetrated the mind, and has been assimilated, than if, in the crises of life, a man recurs to the great thoughts and images of the literature in which he has been trained, and finds there what braces and fortifies him, a comfort, an inspiration, an utterance for his deeper feelings."

Sir Richard Jebb then quotes a touching story of Lord Granville, who was President of the Council in 1762, and whose last hours were rapidly approaching. In reply to a suggestion that, considering his state of health, some important work should be postponed, he uttered the following impassioned words from the Iliad, spoken by Sarpedon to Glaucus: "Ah, friend, if, once escaped from this battle, we were for ever to be ageless and immortal, I would not myself fight in the foremost ranks, nor would I send thee into the war that giveth men renown; but now,—since ten thousand fates of death beset us every day, and these no mortal may escape or avoid, —now let us go forward."

Such was the discipline of the Greek and Roman classics upon the mind of Lord Granville at a great crisis in his life.

Let us now turn to the story of a Chinese statesman, nourished only upon what has been too hastily stigmatised as "the dry bones of Chinese literature."

Wên T'ien-hsiang was born in A.D. 1236. At the age of twenty-one he came out first on the list of successful candidates for the highest literary degree. Upon the draft-list submitted to the Emperor he had been placed seventh; but his Majesty, after looking over the essays, drew the grand examiner's attention to the originality and excellence of that of Wên T'ien-hsiang, and the examiner—himself a great scholar and no sycophant—saw that the Emperor was right, and altered the places accordingly.

Four or five years later Wên T'ien-hsiang attracted attention by demanding the execution of a statesman who had advised that the Court should quit the capital and flee before the advance of the victorious Mongols. Then followed many years of hard fighting, in the course of which his raw levies were several times severely defeated, and he himself was once taken prisoner by the Mongol general, Bayan, mentioned by Marco Polo. He managed to escape on that occasion; but in 1278 the plague broke out in his camp, and he was again defeated and taken prisoner. He was sent to Peking, and every effort was made to induce him to own allegiance to the Mongol conqueror, but without success. He was kept several years in prison. Here is a well-known poem which he wrote while in captivity:—

"There is in the universe an *Aura*, an influence which permeates all things, and makes them what they are. Below, it shapes forth land and water; above, the sun and the stars. In man it is called spirit; and there is nowhere where it is not.

"In times of national tranquillity, this spirit lies hidden in the harmony which prevails. Only at some great epoch is it manifested widely abroad."

Here Wên T'ien-hsiang recalls, and dwells lovingly upon, a number of historical examples of loyalty and devotion. He then proceeds:—

"Such is this grand and glorious spirit which endureth for all generations; and which, linked with the sun and moon, knows neither beginning nor end. The foundation of all that is great and good in heaven and earth, it is itself born from the everlasting obligations which are due by man to man.

"Alas! the fates were against me; I was without resource. Bound with fetters, hurried away toward the north, death would have been sweet indeed; but that boon was refused.

"My dungeon is lighted by the will-o'-the-wisp alone: no breath of spring cheers the murky solitude in which I dwell. The ox and the barb herd together in one stall: the rooster and the phoenix feed together from one dish. Exposed to mist and dew, I had many times thought to die; and yet, through the seasons of two revolving years, disease hovered around me in vain. The dark, unhealthy soil to me became Paradise itself. For there was that within me which misfortune could not steal away. And so I remained firm, gazing at the white clouds floating over my head, and bearing in my heart a sorrow boundless as the sky.

"The sun of those dead heroes has long since set, but their record is before me still. And, while the wind whistles under the eaves, I open my books and read; and lo! in their presence my heart glows with a borrowed fire."

At length, Wên T'ien-hsiang was summoned into the presence of Kublai Khan, who said to him, "What is it you want?" "By the grace of his late Majesty of the Sung dynasty," he replied, "I became his Majesty's minister. I cannot serve two masters. I only ask to die." Accordingly he was executed, meeting his death with composure, and making a final obeisance toward the south, as though his own sovereign was still reigning in his capital.

May we not then plead that this Chinese statesman, equally with Lord Granville, at a crisis of his life, recurred to the great thoughts and images of the literature in which he had been trained, and found there what braced and fortified him, a comfort, an inspiration, an utterance for his deeper feelings?

Chinese history teems with the names of men who, with no higher source of inspiration than the Confucian Canon, have yet shown that they can nobly live and bravely die.

Han Yü of the eighth and ninth centuries was one of China's most brilliant statesmen and writers, and rose rapidly to the highest offices of State. When once in power, he began to attack abuses, and was degraded and banished. Later on, when the Court, led by a weak Emperor, was going crazy over Buddhism, he presented a scathing Memorial to the Throne, from the effect of which it may well be said that Buddhism has not yet recovered. The Emperor was furious, and Han Yü narrowly escaped with his life. He was banished to the extreme wilds of Kuangtung, not far from the now flourishing Treaty Port of Swatow, where he did so much useful work in civilising the aborigines, that he was finally recalled.

Those wilds have long since disappeared as such, but the memory of Han Yü remains, a treasure for ever. In a temple which contains his portrait, and which is dedicated to him, a grateful posterity has put up a tablet bearing the following legend, "Wherever he passed, he purified."

The last Emperor of the Ming dynasty, which was overthrown by rebels and then supplanted by the Manchus in 1644, was also a man who in the Elysian fields might well hold up his head among monarchs. He seems to have inherited with the throne a legacy of national disorder similar to that which eventually brought about the ruin of Louis XVI of France. With all the best intentions possible, he was unable to stem the tide. Over-taxation brought in its train, as it always does in China, first resistance and then rebellion. The Emperor was besieged in Peking by a rebel army; the Treasury was empty; there were too few soldiers to man the walls; and the capital fell.

On the previous night, the Emperor, who had refused to flee, slew the eldest Princess, commanded the Empress to commit suicide, and sent his three sons into hiding. At dawn the bell was struck for the Court to assemble; but no one came. His Majesty then ascended the well-known hill in the Palace grounds, and wrote a last decree on the lapel of his robe:—

"Poor in virtue, and of contemptible personality, I have incurred the wrath of high Heaven. My ministers have deceived me. I am ashamed to meet my ancestors; and therefore I myself take off my cap of State, and with my hair covering my face, await dismemberment at the hands of you rebels."

Instead of the usual formula, "Respect this!" the Emperor added, "Spare my people!"

He then hanged himself, and the great Ming dynasty was no more.

---

Chinese studies have always laboured under this disadvantage,—that the ludicrous side of China and her civilisation was the one which first attracted the attention of foreigners; and to a great extent it does so still. There was a time when China was regarded as a Land of Opposites, *i.e.* diametrically opposed to us in every imaginable direction. For instance, in China the left hand is the place of honour; men keep their hats on in company; use fans; mount their horses on the off side; begin dinner with fruit and end it with soup; shake their own instead of their friends' hands when meeting; begin at what we call the wrong end of a book and read from right to left down vertical columns; wear white for mourning; have huge visiting-cards instead of small ones; prevent criminals from having their hair cut; regard the south as the standard point of the compass; begin to build a house by putting on the roof first; besides many other nicer distinctions, the mere enumeration of which would occupy much of the time at my disposal.

The other side of the medal, showing the similarities, and even the identities, has been unduly neglected; and yet it is precisely from a study of these similarities and identities that the best results can be expected.

A glance at any good dictionary of classical antiquities will at once reveal the minute and painstaking care with which even the small details of life in ancient Greece have been examined into and discussed. The Chinese have done like work for themselves; and many of their beautifully illustrated dictionaries of archæology would compare not unfavourably with anything we have to show.

There are also many details of modern everyday existence in China which may fairly be quoted to show that Chinese civilisation is not, after all, that comic condition of topsy-turvey-dom which the term usually seems to connote.

The Chinese house may not be a facsimile of a Greek house,—far from it. Still, we may note its position, facing south, in order to have as much sun in winter and as little in summer as possible; its division into men's and women's apartments; the fact that the doors are in two leaves and open inward; the rings or handles on the doors; the portable braziers used in the rooms in cold weather; and the shrines of the household gods;—all of which characteristics are to be found equally in the Greek house.

There are also points of resemblance between the lives led by Chinese and Athenian ladies, beyond the fact that the former occupy a secluded portion of the house. The Chinese do not admit their women to social entertainments, and prefer, as we are told was the case with Athenian husbands, to dine by themselves rather than expose their wives to the gaze of their friends. If the Athenian dame "went out at all, it was to see some religious procession, or to a funeral; and if sufficiently advanced in years she might occasionally visit a female friend, and take breakfast with her."

And so in China, it is religion which breaks the monotony of female life, and collects within the temples, on the various festivals, an array of painted faces and embroidered skirts that present, even to the European eye, a not unpleasing spectacle.

That painting the face was universal among the women of Greece, much after the fashion which we now see in China, has been placed beyond all doubt, the pigments used in both cases being white lead and some kind of vegetable red, with lampblack for the eyebrows.

In marriage, we find the Chinese aiming, like the Greeks, at equality of rank and fortune between the contracting parties, or, as the Chinese put it, in the guise of a household word, at a due correspondence between the doorways of the betrothed couple. As in Greece, so in China, we find the marriage arranged by the parents; the veiled bride; the ceremony of fetching her from her father's house; the equality of man and wife; the toleration of subordinate wives, and many other points of contact.

The same sights and scenes which are daily enacted at any of the great Chinese centres of population seem also to have been enacted in the Athenian market-place, with its simmering kettles of boiled peas and other vegetables, and its chapmen and retailers of all kinds of miscellaneous goods. In both we have the public story-teller, surrounded by a well-packed group of fascinated and eager listeners.

The puppet-shows, ἀγάλματα νευρόσπαστα, which Herodotus tells us were introduced into Greece from Egypt, are constantly to be seen in Chinese cities, and date from the second century B.C.,—a suggestive period, as I shall hope to show later on.

The Chinese say that these puppets originated in China as follows:—

The first Emperor of the Han dynasty was besieged, about 200 B.C., in a northern city, by a vast army of Hsiung-nu, the ancestors of the Huns, under the command of the famous chieftain, Mao-tun. One of the Chinese generals with the besieged Emperor discovered that Mao-tun's wife, who was in command on one side of the city, was an extremely jealous woman; and he forthwith caused a number of wooden puppets, representing beautiful girls and worked by strings, to be exhibited on the wall overlooking the chieftain's camp. At this, we are told, the lady's fears for her husband's fidelity were aroused, and she drew off her forces.

The above account may be dismissed as a tale, in which case we are left with Punch and Judy on our hands.

To return to city sights. The tricks of street-jugglers as witnessed in China seem to be very much those of ancient Greece. In both countries we have such feats as jumping about amongst naked swords, spitting fire from the mouth, and passing a sword down the throat.

Then there are the advertisements on the walls; the mule-carts and mule-litters; the sunshades, or umbrellas, carried by women in Greece, by both sexes in China.

The Japanese language is said to contain no terms of abuse, so refined are the inhabitants of that earthly paradise. The Chinese language more than makes up for this deficiency; and it is certainly curious that, as in ancient

Greece, the names of animals are not frequently used in this connection, with the sole exception of the dog. No Chinaman will stand being called a dog, although he really has a great regard for the animal, as a friend whose fidelity is proof even against poverty.

In the ivory shops in China will be found many specimens of the carver's craft which will bear comparison, for the patience and skill required, with the greatest triumphs of Greek workmen. Both nations have reproduced the human hand in ivory; the Greeks used it as an ornament for a hairpin; the Chinese attach it to a slender rod about a foot and a half in length, and use it as a back-scratcher.

The Chinese drama, which we can only trace vaguely to Central Asian sources, and no farther back than the twelfth century of our era, has some points of contact with the Greek drama. In Greece the plays began at sunrise and continued all day, as they do still on the open-air stages of rural districts in China, in both cases performed entirely by men, without interval between the pieces, without curtain, without prompter, and without any attempt at realism.

As formerly in Greece, so now in China, the words of the play are partly spoken and partly sung, the voice of the actor being, in both countries, of the highest importance. Like the Greek actor before masks were invented, the Chinese actor paints his face, and the thick-soled boot which raises the Chinese tragedian from the ground is very much the counterpart of the cothurnus.

The arrangement by which the Greek gods appeared in a kind of balcony, looking out as it were from the heights of Olympus, is well known to the Chinese stage; while the methodical character of Greek tragic dancing, with the chorus moving right and left, is strangely paralleled in the dances performed at the worship of Confucius in the Confucian temples, details of which may be seen in any illustrated Chinese encyclopædia.

Games with dice are of a high antiquity in Greece; they date in China only from the second century A.D., having been introduced from the West under the name of *shu p'u*, a term which has so far defied identification.

The custom of fighting quails was once a political institution in Athens, and under early dynasties it was a favourite amusement at the Imperial Court of China.

The game of "guess-fingers" is another form of amusement common to both countries. So also is the custom of drinking by rule, under the guidance of a toast-master, with fines of deep draughts of wine to be swallowed by those who fail in capping verses, answering conundrums, recognising quotations; to which may be added the custom of introducing singing-girls toward the close of the entertainment.

At Athens, too, it was customary to begin a drinking-bout with small cups, and resort to larger ones later on, a process which must be familiar to all readers of Chinese novels, wherein, toward the close of the revel, the half-drunken hero invariably calls for more capacious goblets. Neither does the ordinary Chinaman approve of a short allowance of wine at his banquets, as witness the following story, translated from a Chinese book of anecdotes.

A stingy man, who had invited some guests to dinner, told his servant not to fill up their wine-cups to the brim, as is usual. During the meal, one of the guests said to his host, "These cups of yours are too deep; you should have them cut down." "Why so?" inquired the host. "Well," replied the guest, "you don't seem to use the top part for anything."

There is another story of a man who went to dine at a house where the wine-cups were very small, and who, on taking his seat at table, suddenly burst out into groans and lamentations. "What is the matter with you?" cried the host, in alarm. "Ah," replied his guest, "my feelings overcame me. My poor father, when dining with a friend who had cups like yours, lost his life, by accidentally swallowing one."

The water-clock, or *clepsydra*, has been known to the Chinese for centuries. Where did it come from? Is it a mere coincidence that the ancient Greeks used water-clocks?

Is it a coincidence that the Greeks used an abacus, or counting-board, on which the beads slid up and down in vertical grooves, while on the Chinese counting-board the only difference is that the beads slide up and down on vertical rods?

Is it a mere coincidence that the olive should be associated in China, as in Greece, with propitiation? To this day, a Chinaman who wishes to make up a quarrel will send a piece of red paper containing an olive, in token of friendly feeling; and the acceptance of this means that the quarrel is at an end.

The olive was supposed by the Greeks to have been brought by Hercules from the land of the Hyperboreans; the Chinese say it was introduced into China in the second century B.C.

The extraordinary similarities between the Chinese and Pythagorean systems of music place it beyond a doubt that one must have been derived from the other. The early Jesuit fathers declared that the ancient Greeks borrowed their music from the Chinese; but we know now that the music in question did not exist in China until two centuries after its appearance in Greece.

The music of the Confucian age perished, books and instruments together, at the Burning of the Books, in B.C. 212; and we read that in the first part of the second century B.C. the hereditary music-master was altogether ignorant of his art. Where did the new art come from? And how are its Greek characteristics to be accounted for?

There are also equally extraordinary similarities between the Chinese and Greek calendars.

For instance, in B.C. 104 the Chinese adopted a cycle of nineteen years, a period which was found to bring together the solar and the lunar years.

But this is precisely the cycle, ἐννεακαιδεκαετηρίς, said to have been introduced by Meton in the fifth century B.C., and adopted at Athens about B.C. 330.

Have we here another coincidence of no particular importance?

The above list might be very much extended. Meanwhile, the question arises: Are there any records of any kind in China which might lead us to suppose that the Chinese ever came into contact in any way with the civilisation of ancient Greece?

We know from Chinese history that, so far back as the second century B.C., victorious Chinese generals carried their arms far into Central Asia, and succeeded in annexing such distant regions as Khoten, Kokand, and the Pamirs. About B.C. 138 a statesman named Chang Ch'ien was sent on a mission to Bactria, but was taken prisoner by the Hsiung-nu, the forebears of the Huns, and detained in captivity for over ten years. He finally managed to escape, and proceeded to Fergana, and thence on to Bactria, returning home in B.C. 126, after having been once more captured by the Hsiung-nu and again detained for about a year.

Now Bactria was then a Greek kingdom, which had been founded by Diodotus in B.C. 256; and it would appear to have had, already for some time, commercial relations with China, for Chang Ch'ien reported that he had seen Chinese merchandise exposed there in the markets for sale. We farther learn that Chang Ch'ien brought back with him the walnut and the grape, previously unknown in China, and taught his countrymen the art of making wine.

The wine of the Confucian period was like the wine of to-day in China, an ardent spirit distilled from rice. There is no grape-wine in China now, although grapes are plentiful and good. But we know from the poetry which has been preserved to us, as well as from the researches of Chinese archæologists, that grape-wine was largely used in China for many centuries subsequent to the date of Chang Ch'ien; in fact, down to the beginning of the fifteenth century, if not later.

One writer says it was brought, together with the "heavenly horse," from Persia, when the extreme West was opened up, a century or so before the Christian era, as already mentioned.

I must now make what may well appear to be an uncalled-for digression; but it will only be a temporary digression, and will bring us back in a few minutes to the grape, the heavenly horse, and to Persia.

Mirrors seem to have been known to the Chinese from the earliest ages. One authority places them so far back as 2500 B.C. They are at any rate mentioned in the *Odes*, say 800 B.C., and were made of polished copper, being in shape, according to the earliest dictionary, like a large basin.

About one hundred years B.C., a new kind of mirror comes into vogue, called by an entirely new name, not before used. In common with the word previously employed, its indicator is "metal," showing under which kingdom it falls,—*i.e.* a mirror of metal. These new mirrors were small disks of melted metal, highly polished on one side and profusely decorated with carvings on the other,—a description which exactly tallies with that of the ancient Greek mirror. Specimens survived to comparatively recent times, and it is even alleged that many of these old mirrors are in existence still. A large number of illustrations of them are given in the great encyclopædia of the eighteenth century, and the fifth of these, in chronological order, second century B.C., is remarkable as being ornamented with the well-known "key," or Greek pattern, so common in Chinese decoration.

Another is covered with birds flying about among branches of pomegranate laden with fruit cut in halves to show the seeds.

Shortly afterward we come to a mirror so lavishly decorated with bunches of grapes and vine-leaves that the eye is arrested at once. Interspersed with these are several animals, among others the lion, which is unknown in China. The Chinese word for "lion," as I stated in my first lecture, is *shih*, an imitation of the Persian *shír*. There is also a lion's head with a bar in its mouth, recalling the door-handles to temples in ancient Greece. Besides the snake, the tortoise, and the sea-otter, there is what is far more remarkable than any of these, namely, a horse with wings.

On comparing the latter with Pegasus as he appears in sculpture, it is quite impossible to doubt that the Chinese is a copy of the Greek animal. The former is said to have come down from heaven, and was caught, according to tradition, on the banks of a river in B.C. 120.

The name for pomegranate in China is "the Parthian fruit," showing that it was introduced from Parthia, the Chinese equivalent for Parthia being 安息 *Ansik*, which is an easy corruption of the Greek Ἀρσάκης, the first king of Parthia.

The term for grape is admittedly of foreign origin, like the fruit itself. It is 葡萄 *pu t'ou*. Here it is easy to recognise the Greek word Βότρυς, a cluster, or bunch, of grapes.

Similarly, the Chinese word for "radish," 蘿蔔 *lo po*, also of foreign origin, is no doubt a corruption of ῥάφη, it being of course well known that the Chinese cannot pronounce an initial *r*.

There is one term, especially, in Chinese which at once carries conviction as to its Greek origin. This is the term for watermelon. The two Chinese characters chosen to represent the sound mean "Western gourd," *i.e.* the gourd which came from the West. Some Chinese say, on no authority in particular, that it was introduced by the Kitan Tartars; others say that it was introduced by the first Emperor of the so-called Golden Tartars. But the Chinese term is still pronounced *si kua*, which is absolutely identical with the Greek word σικύα, of which Liddell and Scott say, "perhaps the melon." For these three words it would now scarcely be rash to substitute "the watermelon."

We are not on quite such firm ground when we compare the Chinese kalends and ides with similar divisions of the Roman month.

Still it is interesting to note that in ancient China, the first day of every month was publicly proclaimed, a sheep being sacrificed on each occasion; also, that the Latin word *kalendae* meant the day when the order of days was proclaimed.

Further, that the term in Chinese for ides means to look at, to see, because on that day we can see the moon; and also that the Latin word *idus*, the etymology of which has not been absolutely established, may possibly come from the Greek ἰδεῖν "to see," just as *kalendae* comes from καλεῖν "to proclaim."

As to many of the analogies, more or less interesting, to be found in the literatures of China and of Western nations, it is not difficult to say how they got into their Chinese setting.

For instance, we read in the History of the Ming Dynasty, A.D. 1368-1644, a full account of the method by which the Spaniards, in the sixteenth century, managed to obtain first a footing in, and then the sovereignty over, some islands which have now passed under the American flag. The following words, not quite without interest at the present day, are translated from the above-mentioned account of the Philippines:—

"The Fulanghis (*i.e.* the Franks), who at that time had succeeded by violence in establishing trade relations with Luzon (the old name of the Philippines), saw that the nation was weak, and might easily be conquered. Accordingly, they sent rich presents to the king of the country, begging him to grant them a piece of land as big as a bull's hide, for building houses to live in. The king, not suspecting guile, conceded their request, whereupon the Fulanghis cut the hide into strips and joined them together, making many hundreds of ten-foot measures in length; and then, having surrounded with these a piece of ground, called upon the king to stand by his promise. The king was much alarmed; but his word had been pledged, and there was no alternative but to submit. So he allowed them to have the ground, charging a small ground-rent as was the custom. But no sooner had the Fulanghis got the ground than they put up houses and ramparts and arranged their fire-weapons (cannon) and engines of attack. Then, seizing their opportunity, they killed the king, drove out the people, and took possession of the country."

It is scarcely credible that Chinese historians would have recorded such an incident unless some trick of the kind had actually been carried out by the Spaniards, in imitation of the famous classical story of the foundation of Carthage.

A professional writer of marvellous tales who flourished in the seventeenth century tells a similar story of the early Dutch settlers:—

"Formerly, when the Dutch were permitted to trade with China, the officer in command of the coast defences would not allow them, on account of their great numbers, to come ashore. The Dutch begged very hard for the grant of a piece of land such as a carpet would cover; and the officer above mentioned, thinking that this could not be very large, acceded to their request. A carpet was accordingly laid down, big enough for about two people to stand on; but by dint of stretching, it was soon able to accommodate four or five; and so the foreigners went on, stretching and stretching, until at last it covered about an acre, and by and by, with the help of their knives, they had filched a piece of ground several miles in extent."

---

These two stories must have sprung from one and the same source. It is not, however, always so simple a matter to see how other Western incidents found their way into Chinese literature. For instance, there is a popular anecdote to be found in a Chinese jest-book, which is almost word for word with another anecdote in Greek literature:—

A soldier, who was escorting a Buddhist priest, charged with some crime, to a prison at a distance, being very anxious not to forget anything, kept saying over and over the four things he had to think about, viz.: himself, his bundle, his umbrella, and the priest. At night he got drunk, and the Buddhist priest, after first shaving the soldier's head, ran away. When the soldier awaked, he began his formula, "Myself, bundle, umbrella—O dear!" cried he, putting his hands to his head, "the priest has gone. Stop a moment," he added, finding his hands in contact with a bald head, "here's the priest; it is I who have run away."

---

As found in Greek literature, the story, attributed to Hierocles, but probably much later, says that the prisoner was a bald-headed man, a condition which is suggested to the Chinese reader by the introduction of a Buddhist priest.

Whether the Chinese got this story from the Greeks, or the Greeks got it from the Chinese, I do not pretend to know. The fact is that we students of Chinese at the present day know very little beyond the vague outlines of what there is to be known. Students of Greek have long since divided up their subject under such heads as pure scholarship, history, philosophy, archæology, and then again have made subdivisions of these. In the Chinese field nothing of the kind has yet been done. The consequence is that the labourers in that field, compelled to work over a large superficies, are only able to turn out more or less superficial work. The cry is for more students, practical students of the written and colloquial languages, for the purposes of diplomatic intercourse and the development of commerce; and also students of the history, philosophy, archæology, and religions of China, men whose contributions to our present stock of knowledge may throw light upon many important points, which, for lack of workmen, have hitherto remained neglected and unexplored.

# TAOISM

China is popularly supposed to have three religions,—Confucianism, Buddhism, and Taoism.

The first is not, and never has been, a religion, being nothing more than a system of social and political morality; the second is indeed a religion, but an alien religion; only the last, and the least known, is of native growth.

The Chinese themselves get over the verbal difficulty by calling these the Three Doctrines.

There have been, at various epochs, other religions in China, and some still remain; the above, however, is the classification commonly in use, all other religions having been regarded up to recent times as devoid of spiritual importance.

Mahommedanism appeared in China in 628 A.D., and is there to this day, having more than once threatened the stability of the Empire.

In 631 the Nestorian Christians arrived, to become later on a flourishing sect, though all trace of them, beyond their famous Tablet, has long since vanished.

It has also been established in recent years that the Zoroastrians, and subsequently the Manichæans, were in China in these early centuries, but nothing now remains of them except the name, a specially invented character, which was equally applied to both.

In the twelfth century the Jews had a synagogue at K'ai-fêng Fu, in Central China, but it is not absolutely certain when they first reached the country. Some say, immediately after the Captivity; others put it much later. In 1850 several Hebrew rolls of parts of the Pentateuch, in the square character, with vowel-points, were obtained from the above city. There were then no professing Jews to be found, but in recent years a movement has been set on foot to revive the old faith.

Roman Catholicism may be said to have existed in China since the close of the sixteenth century, though there was actually an Archbishop of Peking, Jean de Montecorvino, who died there in 1330.

In the last year of the eighteenth century the first Protestant missionary arrived. The first American missionaries followed in 1830. They found China, as it is now, nominally under the sway of the Three Doctrines.

So much has been written on Confucianism, and so much more on Buddhism, that I propose to confine myself entirely to Taoism, which seems to have attracted too little the attention of the general public. In fact, a quite recent work, which professes to deal among other things with the history of China, omits all discussion of this particular religion.

Taoism is the religion of Tao; as to what Tao is, or what it means, we are told upon the highest authority that it is quite impossible to say. This does not seem a very hopeful beginning; but

"even the weariest river
Winds somewhere safe to sea,"

and I shall therefore make an effort to set before you a clue, which, I trust, will lead toward at any rate a partial elucidation of the mystery.

At some unknown period in remote antiquity, there appears to have lived a philosopher, known to posterity as Lao Tzŭ, who taught men, among other things, to return good for evil. His parentage, birth, and life have been overloaded in the course of centuries with legend. Finally, he is said to have foreseen a national cataclysm, and to have disappeared into the West, leaving behind him a book, now called the *Tao-Tê-Ching*, which, for many reasons, he could not possibly have written.

The little we really know of Lao Tzŭ is gathered from traditional utterances of his, scattered here and there in the works of later disciples of his school. Many of these sayings, though by no means all of them, with much other matter of a totally different character, have been brought together in the form of a treatise, and the heterogeneous whole has been ascribed to Lao Tzŭ himself.

Before proceeding with our examination of Tao, it is desirable to show why this work may safely be regarded as a forgery of a later age.

Attempts have been made, by the simple process of interpolation in classical texts, to prove that Lao Tzŭ lived in the same century as that in which Confucius was born; and also that, when the former was a very old man, the two sages met; and further that the interviews ended very much to the astonishment of Confucius. All this, however, has been set aside by the best native scholarship ever produced in China, as the work of later hands.

Further, there was another philosopher of the same name, who really was contemporary with Confucius, and it is held by many Chinese critics that the two have been confused, perhaps with malice aforethought.

We can only say for certain that after Lao Tzŭ came Confucius—at what interval we do not know. Now, in all the works of Confucius, whether as writer or as editor, and throughout all his posthumously published Discourses, there is not a single word of allusion either to Lao Tzŭ or to this treatise. The alleged interviews have been left altogether unnoticed.

One hundred years after Confucius came Mencius, China's second sage. In all his pages of political advice to feudal nobles, and all his conversations with his disciples, much more voluminous than the Discourses of Confucius, there is equally no allusion to Lao Tzŭ, nor to the treatise.

It has been pointed out by an eminent Chinese critic of the fifteenth and sixteenth centuries, that Mencius spent his life chiefly in attacking the various heterodox systems which then prevailed, such as the extreme altruistic system of Mo Ti and the extreme egoistic system of Yang Chu; and it is urged—in my opinion with overwhelming force—that if the *Tao-Tê-Ching* had existed in the days of Mencius, it must necessarily have been recognised and treated as a mischievous work, likely to alienate men's minds from the one perfect and orthodox teaching—Confucianism.

Chuang Tzŭ, a philosopher of the fourth century B.C., devoted himself to elucidating and illuminating the teaching of Lao Tzŭ. His work, which has survived to the present day, will shortly occupy our attention. For the moment it is only necessary to say that it contains many of the Master's traditional sayings, but never once mentions a treatise.

In the third century B.C. there lived another famous Taoist writer, Han Fei Tzŭ, who devotes the best part of two whole sections of his work to explaining and illustrating the sayings of Lao Tzŭ. Yet he never mentions the treatise. He deals with many sayings of Lao Tzŭ now to be found in the treatise, but he does not take them in the order in which they now stand, and he introduces several others which do not occur at all in the treatise, having apparently been overlooked by the compiler.

In the second century B.C. there lived another famous Taoist writer, Huai-nan Tzŭ, who devotes a long chapter to illustrating the doctrines of Lao Tzŭ. He never mentions a book.

One hundred years B.C. comes the historian Ssŭ-ma Ch'ien, whose brilliant work, the first of the Dynastic Histories, I have already had occasion to bring to your notice. In his brief memoir of Lao Tzŭ, he does mention a book in five thousand and more characters; but he mentions it in such a way as to make it clear beyond all doubt that he himself could never have seen it; and moreover, in addition to the fact that no date is given, either of the birth or death of Lao Tzŭ, the account is so tinged with the supernatural as to raise a strong suspicion that some part of it did not really come from the pen of the great historian.

About two hundred years later appeared the first Chinese dictionary, already alluded to in a previous lecture. This work was intended as a collection of all the written characters known at date of publication; and we can well imagine that, with Lao Tzŭ's short treatise before him, there would be no difficulty in including all the words found therein. Such, however, is not the case. There are many characters in the treatise which are not to be found in the dictionary, and in one particular instance the omission is very remarkable.

Much other internal evidence against the genuineness of this work might here be adduced. I will content myself with a single, and a ludicrous, item, which shows how carelessly it was pieced together.

Sentences occur in the *Tao-Tê-Ching* which positively contain, in addition to some actual words by Lao Tzŭ, words from a commentator's explanation, which have been mistaken by the forger for a part of Lao Tzŭ's own utterance.

Add to this the striking fact that the great mass of Chinese critical scholarship is entirely adverse to the claims put forward on behalf of the treatise,—a man who believes in it as the genuine work of Lao Tzŭ being generally regarded among educated Chinese as an amiable crank, much as many people now regard any one who credits the plays of Shakespeare to Lord Bacon,—and I think we may safely dismiss the question without further ado.

It will be more interesting to turn to any sayings of Lao Tzŭ which we can confidently regard as genuine; and those are such as occur in the writings of some of the philosophers above-mentioned, from which they were evidently collected by a pious impostor, and, with the aid of unmistakable padding, were woven into the treatise, of which we may now take a long leave.

Lao Tzŭ imagined the universe to be informed by an omnipresent, omnipotent Principle, which he called *Tao*. Now this word *Tao* means primarily "a road," "a way"; and Lao Tzŭ's Principle may therefore be conveniently translated by "the Way."

Fearing, however, some confusion from the use of this term, the philosopher was careful to explain that "the way which can be walked upon is not the eternal Way." But he never tells us definitely what the Way is. In one place he says it cannot find expression in words; in another he says, "Those who know do not tell; those who tell do not know."

The latter saying was used by a famous poet as a weapon of ridicule against the treatise. "If those who know," he argued, "do not tell, how comes it that Lao Tzŭ put his own knowledge into a book of five thousand and more words?"

We are assured, however, by Lao Tzŭ that "just as without going out of doors we can know the whole world, so without looking out of window we can know the Way."

Again we have, "Without moving, you shall know; without looking, you shall see; without doing, you shall achieve."

Meanwhile, we are left to gather from isolated maxims some shadowy idea of what Lao Tzŭ meant by the Way.

It seems to have been a perpetual accommodation of self to one's surroundings, with the minimum of effort, all progress being spontaneous and in the line of least resistance.

From this it is a mere step to doing nothing at all, the famous doctrine of Inaction, with all its paradoxes, which is really the criterion of Lao Tzŭ's philosophy and will be always associated with Lao Tzŭ's name.

Thus he says, "Perfect virtue does nothing, and consequently there is nothing which it does not do."

Again, "The softest things in the world overcome the hardest; that which has no substance enters where there is no crevice."

"Leave all things to take their natural courses, and do not interfere."

"Only he who does nothing for his life's sake can be truly said to value his life."

"Govern a great nation as you would cook a small fish,"—do not overdo it. Do not try to force results. The well-known Greek injunction, "not to go beyond one's destiny," οὐκ ὑπὲρ μόρον, might well have fallen from Lao Tzŭ's lips.

All this is the Way, which Lao Tzŭ tells us is "like the drawing of a bow,—it brings down the high and exalts the low," reducing all things to a uniform plane.

He also says that if the Way prevails on earth, horses will be used for agricultural purposes; if the Way does not prevail, they will be used for war.

Many of Lao Tzŭ's sayings are mere moral maxims for use in everyday life.

"Put yourself behind, and the world will put you in front; put yourself in front, and the world will put you behind."

"To the good I would be good; to the not-good I would also be good, in order to make them good."

All together, with the comparatively few scraps of Lao Tzŭ's wisdom to be found in the treatise, we should be hard put to understand the value of Tao, and still more to find sufficient basis for a philosophical system, were it not for his disciple, Chuang Tzŭ, of the fourth century B.C., who produced a work expanding and illustrating the Way of his great Master, so rich in thought and so brilliant from a literary point of view that, although branded since the triumph of Confucianism with the brand of heterodoxy, it still remains a storehouse of current quotation and a model of composition for all time.

Let us go back to *Tao*, in which, Chuang Tzŭ tells us, man is born, as fishes are born in water; for, as he says in another place, there is nowhere where *Tao* is not. But *Tao* cannot be heard; heard, it is not *Tao*. It cannot be seen; seen, it is not *Tao*. It cannot be spoken; spoken, it is not *Tao*. Although it imparts form, it is itself formless, and cannot therefore have a name, since form precedes name.

The unsubstantiality of *Tao* is further dwelt upon as follows:—

"Were *Tao* something which could be presented, there is no man but would present it to his sovereign or to his parents. Could it be imparted or given, there is no man but would impart it to his brother or give it to his child. But this is impossible. For unless there is a suitable endowment within, *Tao* will not abide; and unless there is outward correctness, *Tao* will not operate."

It would seem therefore that *Tao* is something which altogether transcends the physical senses of man and is correspondingly difficult of attainment. Chuang Tzŭ comes thus to the rescue:—

"By absence of thought, by absence of cogitation, *Tao* may be known. By resting in nothing, by according in nothing, *Tao* may be approached. By following nothing, by pursuing nothing, *Tao* may be attained."

What there was before the universe, was *Tao*. *Tao* makes things what they are, but is not itself a thing. Nothing can produce *Tao*; yet everything has Tao within it, and continues to produce it without end.

"Rest in Inaction," says Chuang Tzŭ, "and the world will be good of itself. Cast your slough. Spit forth intelligence. Ignore all differences.

Become one with the Infinite. Release your mind. Free your soul. Be vacuous. Be nothing!"

Chuang Tzŭ lays especial emphasis on the cultivation of the natural as opposed to the artificial.

"Horses and oxen have four feet; that is the natural. Put a halter on a horse's head, a string through a bullock's nose; that is the artificial."

"A drunken man who falls out of a cart, though he may suffer, does not die. His bones are the same as other people's; but he meets his accident in a different way. His spirit is in a condition of security. He is not conscious of riding in the cart; neither is he conscious of falling out of it. Ideas of life, death, fear, etc., cannot penetrate his breast; and so he does not suffer from contact with objective existences. And if such security is to be got from wine, how much more is it to be got from *Tao*?"

The doctrine of Relativity in space and time, which Chuang Tzŭ deduces from Lao Tzŭ's teachings, is largely introduced by the disciple.

"There is nothing under the canopy of Heaven greater than an autumn spikelet. A vast mountain is a small thing. The universe and I came into being together; and all things therein are One.

"In the light of *Tao*, affirmative is reconciled with negative; objective is identified with subjective. And when subjective and objective are both without their correlates, that is the very axis of *Tao*. And when that axis passes through the centre at which all infinities converge, positive and negative alike blend into an infinite One."

Thus, morally speaking, we can escape from the world and self, and can reverse and look down upon the world's judgments; while in the speculative region we get behind and beyond the contradictions of ordinary thought and speech. A perfect man is the result. He becomes, as it were, a spiritual being. As Chuang Tzŭ puts it:—

"Were the ocean itself scorched up, he would not feel hot. Were the Milky Way frozen hard, he would not feel cold. Were the mountains to be riven with thunder, and the great deep to be thrown up by storm, he would not tremble. In such case, he would mount upon the clouds of Heaven, and driving the sun and moon before him, would pass beyond the limits of this external world, where death and life have no more victory over man."

We have now an all-embracing One, beyond the limits of this world, and we have man perfected and refined until he is no longer a prey to objective existences. Lao Tzŭ has already hinted at "the Whence, and oh, Heavens, the Whither." He said that to emerge was life, and to return was death. Chuang Tzŭ makes it clear that what man emerges from is some transcendental state in the Infinite; and that to the Infinite he may ultimately return.

"How," he asks, "do I know that love of life is not a delusion after all? How do I know that he who dreads to die is not like a child who has lost the way, and cannot find his home?

"Those who dream of the banquet wake to lamentation and sorrow. Those who dream of lamentation and sorrow wake to join the hunt. While they dream, they do not know that they dream. Some will even interpret the very dream they are dreaming; and only when they awake do they know it was a dream. By and by comes the Great Awakening, and then we find out that this life is really a great dream. Fools think they are awake now, and flatter themselves they know if they are really princes or peasants. Confucius and you are both mere dreams; and I, who say you are dreams,—I am but a dream myself.

"Take no heed," he adds, "of time, nor of right and wrong; but passing into the realm of the Infinite, find your final rest therein."

An abstract Infinite, however, soon ceased to satisfy the natural cravings of the great body of Taoist followers. Chuang Tzŭ had already placed the source of human life beyond the limits of our visible universe; and in order to secure a return thither, it was only necessary to refine away the grossness of our material selves according to the doctrine of the Way. It thus came about that the One, in whose obliterating unity all seemingly opposed conditions were to be indistinguishably blended, began to be regarded as a fixed point of dazzling intellectual luminosity, in remote ether, around which circled for ever and ever, in the supremest glory of motion, the souls of those who had successfully passed through the ordeal of life, and who had left the slough of humanity behind them.

Let me quote some lines from a great Taoist poet, Ssŭ-k'ung T'u, written to support this view. His poem consists of twenty-four stanzas, each twelve lines in length, and each dealing with some well-known phase of Taoist doctrine.

"Expenditure of force leads to outward decay,
Spiritual existence means inward fulness.
Let us revert to Nothing and enter the Absolute,
Hoarding up strength for Energy.
Freighted with eternal principles,
Athwart the mighty void,
Where cloud-masses darken,
And the wind blows ceaseless around,
Beyond the range of conceptions,
Let us gain the Centre,
And there hold fast without violence,
Fed from an inexhaustible supply."

In this, the first, stanza we are warned against taxing, or even using, our physical powers, instead of aiming, as we should, at a purely spiritual existence, by virtue of which we shall ultimately be wafted away to the distant Centre in the Infinite.

"Lo, the Immortal, borne by spirituality,
His hand grasping a lotus-flower,
Away to Time everlasting,
Trackless through the regions of Space!"

These four lines from stanza v give us a glimpse of the liberated mortal on his upward journey. The lotus-flower, which the poet has placed in his hand, is one of those loans from Buddhism to which I shall recur by and by.

"As iron from the mines,
As silver from lead,
So purify thy heart,
Loving the limpid and clean.
Like a clear pool in spring,
With its wondrous mirrored shapes,

So make for the spotless and true,
And riding the moonbeam revert to the Spiritual."

These eight lines from stanza vii, which might be entitled "Smelting," show us the refining process by which spirituality is to be attained.

Seclusion and abandonment of the artificial are also extolled in stanza xv: —

"Following our own bent,
Let us enjoy the Natural, free from curb,
Rich with what comes to hand,
Hoping some day to be with the Infinite.
To build a hut beneath the pines,
With uncovered head to pore over poetry,
Knowing only morning and eve,
But not what season it may be ...
Then, if happiness is ours
Why must there be Action?
If of our own selves we can reach this point,
Can we not be said to have attained?"

Utterances of this kind are responsible for the lives of many Taoist hermits who from time to time have withdrawn from the world, devoting themselves to the pursuit of true happiness, on the mountains.

"After gazing abstractedly upon expression and substance,
The mind returns with a spiritual image,
As when seeking the outlines of waves,
As when painting the glory of spring.
The changing shapes of wind-swept clouds,
The energies of flowers and plants,
The rolling breakers of ocean,
The crags and cliffs of mountains,
All these are like mighty TAO,
Skilfully woven into earthly surroundings ...
To obtain likeness without form
Is not that to possess the man?"

This stanza means that man should become like the contour of waves, like the glory of spring,—something which to a beholder is a mental image, without constant physical form or substance. Then motion supervenes; not motion as we know it, but a transcendental state of revolution in the Infinite. This is the subject of stanza xxiv:—

"Like a whirling water-wheel,
Like rolling pearls,—
Yet how are these worthy to be named?
They are but adaptations for fools.
There is the mighty axis of Earth,
The never resting pole of Heaven;
Let us grasp *their* clue,
And with *them* be blended in One,
Beyond the bounds of thought,
Circling for ever in the great Void,
An orbit of a thousand years,—
Yes, this is the key to my theme."

All that might be dignified by the name of pure Taoism ends here. From this point the descent to lower regions is both easy and rapid.

I am not speaking now in a chronological sense, but of the highest intellectual point reached by the doctrines of Taoism, which began to decline long before the writer of this poem, himself a pure Taoist of the tenth century, was born.

The idea mentioned above, that the grosser elements of man's nature might be refined away and immortality attained, seems to have suggested an immortality, not merely in an unseen world, but even in this one, to be secured by an imaginary elixir of life. Certain at any rate it is, that so far back as a century or so before the Christian era, the desire to discover this elixir had become a national craze.

The following story is historical, and dates from about 200 B.C.:—

"A certain person having forwarded some elixir of immortality to the Prince of Ching, it was received as usual by the doorkeeper. 'Is this to be swallowed?' enquired the Chief Warden of the palace. 'It is,' replied the doorkeeper. Thereupon, the Chief Warden purloined and swallowed it. At this, the Prince was exceedingly angry and ordered his immediate execution; but the Chief Warden sent a friend to plead for him, saying, 'Your Highness's servant asked the doorkeeper if the drug was to be swallowed, and as he replied in the affirmative, your servant accordingly swallowed it. The blame rests entirely with the doorkeeper. Besides, if the elixir of life is presented to your Highness, and because your servant swallows it, your Highness slays him, that elixir is clearly the elixir of death; and for your Highness thus to put to death an innocent official is simply for your Highness to be made the sport of men.' The Prince spared his life."

The later Taoist was not content with attempts to compound an elixir. He invented a whole series of physical exercises, consisting mostly of positions, or postures, in which it was necessary to sit or stand, sometimes for an hour or so at a time, in the hope of prolonging life. Such absurdities as swallowing the saliva three times in every two hours were also held to be conducive to long life.

There is perhaps more to be said for a system of deep breathing, especially of morning air, which was added on the strength of the following passage in Chuang Tzŭ:—

"The pure men of old slept without dreams, and waked without anxiety. They ate without discrimination, breathing deep breaths. For pure men draw breath from their uttermost depths; the vulgar only from their throats."

A Chinese official with whom I became acquainted in the island of Formosa was outwardly a Confucianist, but inwardly a Taoist of the deepest dye. He used to practise the above exercises and deep breathing in his spare moments, and strongly urged me to try them. Apparently they were no safeguard against malarial fever, of which he died about a year or so afterward.

Associated closely with the elixir of immortality is the practice of alchemy, which beyond all doubt was an importation from Greece by way of Bactria.

We read in the Historical Record, under date 133 B.C., of a man who appeared at court and persuaded the Emperor that gold could be made out of cinnabar or red sulphide of mercury; and that if dishes made of the gold thus produced were used for food, the result would be prolongation of life, even to immortality. He pretended to be immortal himself; and when he died, as he did within the year, the infatuated Emperor believed, in the words of the historian, "that he was only transfigured and not really dead," and accordingly gave orders to continue the experiments.

For many centuries the attempt to turn base metal into gold occupied a leading place in the researches of Chinese philosophers. Volumes have been written on the subject, and are still studied by a few.

The best-known of these has been attributed to a Taoist hermit who flourished in the second century A.D., and was summoned to court, but refused the invitation, being, as he described himself, a lowly man, living simply, and with no love for power and glory. The work in question was actually mistaken for a commentary on the *Book of Changes*, mentioned in a former lecture, though it is in reality a treatise upon alchemy, and also upon the concoction of pills of immortality. It was forwarded to me some years ago by a gentleman in America, with a request that I would translate it as a labour of love; but I was obliged to decline what seemed to me a useless task, especially as the book was really written by another man, of the same name as the hermit, who lived more than twelve hundred years later.

The author is said to have ultimately succeeded in compounding these pills of immortality, and to have administered one by way of experiment to a dog, which at once fell down dead. He then swallowed one himself, with the same result; whereupon his elder brother, with firm faith, and undismayed by what he saw before him, swallowed a third pill. The same fate overtook him, and this shook the confidence of a remaining younger brother, who went off to make arrangements for burying the bodies. But by the time he had returned the trio had recovered, and were straightway enrolled among the ranks of the immortals.

As another instance of the rubbish in which the modern Taoist delights to believe, I may quote the story of the Prince of Huai-nan, second century

B.C., who is said, after years of patient experiment, to have finally discovered the elixir of life. Immediately on tasting the drug, his body became imponderable, and he began to rise heavenward. Startled probably by this new sensation, he dropped the cup out of which he had been drinking, into the courtyard; whereupon his dogs and poultry finished up the dregs, and were soon sailing up to heaven after him.

It was an easy transition from alchemy and the elixir of life to magic and the black art in general. Those Taoists who, by their manner of life, or their reputed successes in the above two fields of research, attracted public attention, came to be regarded as magicians or wizards, in communication with, and in control of, the unseen powers of darkness. The accounts of their combats with evil spirits, to be found in many of the lower-class novels, are eagerly devoured by the Chinese, who even now frequently call in Taoist priests to exorcise some demon which is supposed to be exerting an evil influence on the family.

As a specimen, there is a story of a young man who had fallen under the influence of a beautiful young girl, when he met a Taoist priest in the street, who started on seeing him, and said that his face showed signs that he had been bewitched. Hurrying home, the young man found his door locked; and on creeping softly up to the window and looking in, he saw a hideous devil, with a green face and jagged teeth like a saw, spreading a human skin on the bed, and painting it with a paint-brush. The devil then threw aside the brush, and giving the skin a shake-out, just as you would a coat, cast it over its shoulders, when lo! there stood the girl.

The story goes on to say that the devil-girl killed the young man, ripping him open and tearing out his heart; after which the priest engaged in terrible conflict with her. Finally—and here we seem to be suddenly transported to the story of the fisherman in the *Arabian Nights*—she became a dense column of smoke curling up from the ground, and then the priest took from his vest an uncorked gourd, and threw it right into the midst of the smoke. A sucking noise was heard, and the whole column was drawn into the gourd; after which the priest corked it up closely, and carried it away with him.

The search for the elixir of life was too fascinating to be readily given up. It was carried on with more or less vigour for centuries, as we learn from the following Memorial to the Throne, dating from the ninth century A.D., presented by an aggrieved Confucianist:—

"Of late years the court has been overrun by a host of 'professors,' who pretend to have the secret of immortality.

"Now supposing that such beings as immortals really did exist—would they not be likely to hide themselves in deep mountain recesses, far from the ken of man? On the other hand, persons who hang about the vestibules of the rich and great, and brag of their wonderful powers in big words,—what are they more than common adventurers in search of pelf? How should their nonsense be credited, and their drugs devoured? Besides, even medicines to cure bodily ailments are not to be swallowed casually, morning, noon, and night. How much less, then, this poisonous, fiery gold-stone, which the viscera of man must be utterly unable to digest?"

Thus gradually Taoism lost its early simple characteristics associated with the name of Lao Tzŭ. The *Tao* developed by Chuang Tzŭ, in the light of which all things became one, paved the way for One Concrete Ruler of the universe; and the dazzling centre, far away in space, became the heaven which was to be the resting-place of virtuous mortals after death. Then came Buddhism, with its attractive ritual and its manifold consolations, and put an end once for all to the ancient glories of the teachings of Lao Tzŭ.

The older text-books date the first appearance of Buddhism in China from 67 A.D., when in consequence of a dream the reigning Emperor sent a mission to the West, and was rewarded by obtaining copies of parts of the Canon, brought to China by Kashiapmadunga, an Indian priest, who, after translating a portion into Chinese, fell ill and died.

But we know now that Buddhist monks had already appeared in China so early as 230 B.C. The monks were thrown into prison, but were said to have been released in the night by an angel.

Still, it was not until the third or fourth century of our era that the new religion began to make itself appreciably felt. "When this came about, there ensued a long and fierce struggle between the Buddhists and the Taoists, resulting, after alternating triumphs and defeats on both sides, in that mutual toleration which obtains at the present day.

Each religion began early to borrow from the other. In the words of the philosopher Chu Hsi, of the eleventh century, "Buddhism stole the best features of Taoism; Taoism stole the worst features of Buddhism. It is as though one took a jewel from the other, and the loser recouped the loss with a stone."

From Buddhism the Taoists borrowed their whole scheme of temples, priests, nuns, and ritual. They drew up liturgies to resemble the Buddhist *sûtras*; and also prayers for the dead. They adopted the idea of a Trinity, consisting of Lao Tzŭ, the mythological Adam of China, and the Ruler of the Universe, before mentioned; and they further appropriated the Buddhist Purgatory with all its frightful terrors and tortures after death.

Nowadays it takes an expert to distinguish between the temples and priests of the two religions, and members of both hierarchies are often simultaneously summoned by persons needing religious consolation or ceremonial of any kind.

The pure and artless *Tao* of Lao Tzŭ, etherealised by the lofty speculations of Chuang Tzŭ, has long since become the vehicle of base and worthless superstition.

# SOME CHINESE MANNERS AND CUSTOMS

A foreigner arriving for the first time in China will be especially struck by three points to which he is not accustomed at home.

The people will consist almost entirely of men; they will all wear their hair plaited in queues; and they will all be exactly alike.

The seclusion of women causes the traveller least surprise of the three, being a custom much more rigorously enforced in other Oriental countries; and directly he gets accustomed to the uniform absence of beard and moustache, he soon finds out that the Chinese people are not one whit more alike facially than his own countrymen of the West.

A Chinaman cannot wear a beard before he is forty, unless he happens to have a married son. He also shaves the whole head with the exception of a round patch at the back, from which the much-prized queue is grown.

There are some strange misconceptions as to the origin and meaning of the queue, more perhaps on the other side of the Atlantic, where we are not so accustomed to Chinamen as you are in America. Some associate the queue with religion, and gravely state that without it no Chinaman could be hauled into Paradise. Others know that queues have only been worn by the Chinese for about two hundred and fifty years, and that they were imposed as a badge of conquest by the Manchu-Tartars, the present rulers of China. Previous to 1644 the Chinese clothed their bodies and dressed their hair in the style of the modern Japanese,—of course I mean those Japanese who still wear what is wrongly known as "the beautiful native dress of Japan,"—wrongly, because as a matter of fact the Japanese borrowed their dress, as well as their literature, philosophy, and early lessons in art, from China. The Japanese dress is the dress of the Ming period in China, 1368-1644.

It remains still to be seen whence and wherefore the Manchu-Tartars obtained this strange fashion of the queue.

The Tartars may be said to have depended almost for their very existence upon the horse; and in old pictures the Tartar is often seen lying curled up asleep with his horse, illustrating the mutual affection and dependence between master and beast. Out of sheer gratitude and respect for his noble ally, the man took upon himself the form of the animal, growing a queue in imitation of the horse's tail.

Unsupported by any other evidence, this somewhat grotesque theory would fall to the ground. But there *is* other evidence, of a rather striking character, which, taken in conjunction with what has been said, seems to me to settle the matter.

Official coats, as seen in China at the present day, are made with very peculiar sleeves, shaped like a horse's leg, and ending in what is an unmistakable hoof, completely covering the hand. These are actually known to the Chinese as "horse-shoe sleeves"; and, encased therein, a Chinaman's arms certainly look very much like a horse's forelegs. The tail completes the picture.

When the Tartars conquered China two hundred and fifty years ago, there was at first a strenuous fight against the queue, and it has been said that the turbans still worn by the Southern Chinese were originally adopted as a means of concealing the hateful Manchu badge. Nowadays every Chinaman looks upon his queue as an integral and honourable part of himself. If he cannot grow one, he must have recourse to art, for he could not appear tailless, either in this world or the next.

False queues are to be seen hanging in the streets for sale. They are usually worn by burglars, and come off in your hand when you think you have caught your man. Prisoners are often led to, and from, gaol by their queues, sometimes three or four being tied together in a gang.

False hair is not confined entirely to the masculine queue. Chinese ladies often use it as a kind of chignon; and it is an historical fact that a famous Empress, who set aside the Emperor and ruled China with an Elizabethan hand from A.D. 684 to 705, used to present herself in the Council Chamber, before her astonished ministers, fortified by an artificial beard.

Dyeing the hair, too, has been practised in China certainly from the Christian era, if not earlier, chiefly by men whose hair and beards begin to grow grey too soon. One of the proudest titles of the Chinese, carrying them back as it does to prehistoric times, is that of the Black-haired People, also a title, perhaps a mere coincidence, of the ancient Accadians. In spite, however, of the universality of black hair in both men and women, there are exceptions to the rule, and I myself have seen a Chinese albino, with the usual light-coloured hair and pink eyes.

---

The Rev. Dr. Arthur Smith, an American missionary, has long been known for his keen insight into the workings of the Chinese mind. In his last book, *China in Convulsion*, under the head of "Protestant Missions," he makes the following important statement,—important not only to those who intend to take part in missionary work, but also to the official, to the explorer, and to the merchant:—

"It would be unfair," he says, "not to point out that when a large body of Occidentals, imperfectly acquainted with the Chinese language, etiquette, modes of thought, and intellectual presuppositions, begins on a large and universal scale the preaching of an uncompromising system of morals and doctrines like Christianity, there must be much which, unconsciously to themselves, rouses Chinese prejudices."

The following maxim comes from Confucius:—

"If you visit a foreign State, ask what the prohibitions are; if you go into a strange neighbourhood, enquire what the manners and customs are." Certainly it is altogether desirable that a foreigner going to China, whether in an official capacity, or as merchant, missionary, or traveller, should have some acquaintance with the ordinary rules and ceremonial of Chinese social life. Such knowledge will often go far to smooth away Chinese prejudices against the barbarian, and on occasions might conceivably aid in averting a catastrophe.

It is true that Lao Tzŭ said, "Ceremonies are but the veneer of loyalty and good faith." His words, however, have not prevailed against the teaching of Confucius, who was an ardent believer in the value of ceremonial. One of the latter's disciples wished, as a humanitarian, to abolish the sacrifice of a sheep upon the first day of every month; but Confucius rebuked him, saying, "My son, you love the sheep; I love the ceremony."

When, during his last visit to England, Li Hung-chang made remarks about Mr. Chamberlain's eyeglass, he was considered by many to be wanting in common politeness. But from the Chinese point of view it was Mr. Chamberlain who was offending—quite unwittingly, of course—against an important canon of good taste. It is a distinct breach of Chinese etiquette to wear spectacles while speaking to an equal. The Chinese invariably remove their glasses when conversing; for what reason I have never been able to discover. One thing is quite certain: they do not like being looked at through a medium of glass or crystal, and it costs the foreigner nothing to fall in with their harmless prejudice.

Chinese street etiquette is also quite different from our own, a fact usually ignored by blustering foreigners, who march through a Chinese town as if the place belonged to them, and not infrequently complain that coolies and others will not "get out of their way." Now there is a graduated scale of Chinese street rights in this particular respect, to which, as being recognised by the Chinese themselves, it would be advisable for foreigners to pay some attention. In England it has been successfully maintained that the roadway belongs to all equally, foot-passengers, equestrians, and carriage-passengers alike. Not so in China; the ordinary foot-passenger is bound to "get out of the way" of the lowest coolie who is carrying a load; that same coolie must make way, even at great inconvenience to himself, for a sedan-chair; an empty chair yields the way to a chair with somebody inside; a chair, inasmuch as being more manageable, gets out of the way of a horse; and horse, chair, coolie, and foot-passenger, all clear the road for a wedding or other procession, or for the retinue of a mandarin.

At the same time a Chinaman may stop his cart or barrow, or dump down his load, just where-ever he pleases, and other persons have to make the best of what is left of the road. I have even seen a theatrical stage built right across a street, completely blocking it, so that all traffic had to be diverted from its regular course. There are no municipal regulations and no police in China, so that the people have to arrange things among themselves; and, considering the difficulties inherent in such an absence of government, it may fairly be said that they succeed remarkably well.

When two friends meet in the street, either may put up his fan and screen his face; whereupon the other will pass by without a sign of recognition. The meaning is simply, "Too busy to stop for a chat," and the custom, open and above-board as it is, compares favourably perhaps with the "Not at home" of Western civilisation.

I do not know of any Chinese humorist who ever, as in the old story, shouted out to a visitor, "I am not at home." Confucius himself certainly came very near to doing so. It is on record that when an unwelcome visitor came to call, the sage sent out to say that he was too ill to receive guests, at the same time seizing his harpsichord and singing to it from an open window, in order to expose the hollowness of his own plea.

Any one on horseback, or riding in a sedan-chair, who happens to meet a friend walking, must dismount before venturing to salute him. However to obviate the constant inconvenience of so doing, the foot-passenger is in duty bound to screen his face as above; and thus, by a fiction which deceives nobody, much unnecessary trouble is saved.

When two mandarins of equal rank find themselves face to face in their sedan-chairs, those attendants among their retinues who carry the enormous wooden fans rush forward and insert these between the passing chairs, so that their masters may be presumed not to see each other and consequently not be obliged to get out.

No subordinate can ever meet a higher mandarin in this way; the former must turn down some by-street immediately on hearing the approaching gong of his superior officer. A mandarin's rank can be told by the number of consecutive strokes on the gong, ranging from thirteen for a viceroy to seven for a magistrate.

Take the case of a Chinese visitor. He should be received at the front door, and be conducted by the host to a reception-room, the host being careful to see that the visitor is always slightly in advance. The act of sitting down should be simultaneous, so that neither party is standing while the other is seated. If the host wishes to be very attentive, he may take a cup of tea from his servant's hands and himself arrange it for his guest.

Here comes another most important and universal rule: in handing anything to, or receiving anything from, an equal both hands must be used. A servant should hand a cup of tea with both hands, except when serving his master and a guest. Then he takes one cup in each hand, and hands them with the arms crossed. I was told that the crossing was in order to exhibit to each the "heart," *i.e.* the palm, of the hand, in token of loyalty.

There is a curious custom in connection with the invariable cup of tea served to a visitor on arrival which is often violated by foreigners, to the great amusement of the Chinese. The tea in question, known as guest-tea, is not intended for ordinary drinking purposes, for which wine is usually provided. No sooner does the guest raise the cup of tea to his lips, or even touch it with his hand, than a shout is heard from the servants, which means that the interview is at an end and that the visitor's sedan-chair is to be got ready. Drinking this tea is, in fact, a signal for departure. A host may similarly, without breach of good manners, be the first to drink, and thus delicately notify the guest that he has business engagements elsewhere.

Then again, it is the rule to place the guest at one's left hand, though curiously enough this only dates from the middle of the fourteenth century, previous to which the right hand was the place of honour.

Finally, when the guest takes his leave, it is proper to escort him back to the front door. That, at any rate, is sufficient, though it is not unusual to accompany a guest some part of his return journey. In fact, the Chinese proverb says, "If you escort a man at all, escort him all the way." This, however, is rhetorical rather than practical, somewhat after the style of another well-known Chinese proverb, "If you bow at all, bow low."

A Chinese invitation to dinner differs somewhat from a similar compliment in the West. You will receive a red envelope containing a red card,—red being the colour associated with festivity,—on which it is stated that by noon on a given day the floor will be swept, the wine-cups washed, and your host in waiting to meet your chariot. Later on, a second invitation will arrive, couched in the same terms; and again another on the day of the banquet, asking you to be punctual to the minute. To this you pay no attention, but make preparations to arrive about 4 P.M., previous to which another and more urgent summons may very possibly have been sent. All this is conventional, and the guests assemble at the same hour, to separate about 9 P.M.

Women take no part in Chinese social entertainments except among their own sex. It is not even permissible to enquire after the wife of one's host. Her very existence is ignored. A man will talk with pleasure about his children, especially if his quiver is well stocked with boys.

In this connection I may say that the position of women in China still seems to be very widely misunderstood. Not only that, but a very frightful crime is alleged against the Chinese people as a common practice in everyday life, which, if not actually approved, meets everywhere with toleration.

I allude to the charge of infanticide, confined of course to girls, for it has not often been suggested that Chinese parents do away with such a valuable asset as a boy.

Miss Gordon Cumming, the traveller, in her *Wanderings in China*, has the following impassioned paragraph in reference to her visit to Ningpo:—

"The delicate fragrance (of the roses and honeysuckle), alas! cannot overpower the appalling odours which here and there assail us, poisoning the freshness of the evening breezes.

"These are wafted from the Baby Towers, two of which we had to pass. These are square towers, with small windows, about twelve feet from the ground, somewhat resembling pigeon-towers; these strange dove-cotes are built to receive the bodies of such babies as die too young to have fully developed souls, and therefore there is no necessity to waste coffins on them, or even to take the trouble of burying them in the bosom of mother earth. So the insignificant little corpse is handed over to a coolie, who, for the sum of forty *cash*, equal to about five cents, carries it away, ostensibly to throw it into one of these towers; but if he should not choose to go so far, he gets rid of it somehow,—no questions are asked, and there are plenty of prowling dogs ever on the watch seeking what they may devour. To-day several poor uncoffined mites were lying outside the towers, shrouded only in a morsel of old matting—apparently they had been brought by some one who had failed to throw them in at the window ('about twelve feet from the ground'), in which, by the way, one had stuck fast!

"Some of these poor little creatures are brought here alive and left to die, and some of these have been rescued and carried to foundling hospitals. The neighbourhood was so pestiferous that we could only pause a moment to look at 'an institution' which, although so horrible, is so characteristic of this race, who pay such unbounded reverence to the powerful dead who could harm them. Most of the bodies deposited here are those of girl babies who have been intentionally put to death, but older children are often thrown in."

With regard to this, I will only say that I lived all together for over four years within a mile or so of these Towers, which I frequently passed during the evening walk; and so far from ever seeing "several poor uncoffined mites lying outside the towers, shrouded only in a morsel of old matting," which Miss Gordon Cumming has described, I never even saw one single instance of a tower being put to the purpose for which it was built, viz.: as a burying-place for the dead infants of people too poor to spend money upon a grave. As for living children being thrown in, I think I shall be able to dispose of that statement a little later on. Miss Gordon Cumming did not add that these towers are cleared out at regular intervals by a Chinese charitable society which exists for that purpose, the bodies burnt, and the ashes reverently buried.

Mrs. Bird-Bishop, the traveller, is reported to have stated at a public lecture in 1897, that "one of the most distressing features of Chinese life was the contempt for women. Of eleven Bible-women whom she had seen at a meeting in China, there was not one who had not put an end to at least five girl-babies."

A Jesuit missionary has published a quarto volume, running to more than 270 pages, and containing many illustrations of infanticide, and the judgments of Heaven which always come upon those who commit this crime.

Finally, if you ask of any Chinaman, he will infallibly tell you that infanticide exists to an enormous extent everywhere in China; and as though in corroboration of his words, alongside many a pool in South China may be found a stone tablet bearing an inscription to the effect that "Female children may not be drowned here." This would appear to end the discussion; but it does not.

To begin with, the Chinese are very prone to exaggerate, especially to foreigners, even their vices. They seem to think that some credit may be extracted from anything, provided it is on a sufficiently imposing scale, and I do not at all doubt the fact that eleven Bible-women told Mrs. Bird-Bishop that they had each destroyed five girl-babies. It is just what I should have expected. I remember, when I first went to Amoy, it had been stated in print by a reckless foreigner that crucifixion of a most horrible kind was one of the common punishments of the place. On enquiring from the Chinese writer attached to the Consulate, the man assured me that the story was quite true and that I could easily see for myself. I told him that I was very anxious to do so, and promised him a hundred dollars for the first case he might bring to my notice. Three years later I left Amoy, with the hundred dollars still unclaimed.

Further, those Chinese who have any money to spare are much given to good works, chiefly, I feel bound to add, in view of the recompense their descendants will receive in this world and they themselves in the next; also, because a rich man who does nothing in the way of charity comes to be regarded with disapprobation by his poorer neighbours. Such persons print and circulate gratis all kinds of religious tracts, against gambling, wine-drinking, opium-smoking, infanticide, and so forth; and these are the persons who set up the stone tablets above-mentioned, regardless whether infanticide happens to be practised or not.

Of course infanticide is known in China, just as it is known, too well known, in England and elsewhere. What I hope to be able to show is that infanticide is not more prevalent in China than in the Christian communities of the West.

Let me begin by urging, what no one who has lived in China will deny, that Chinese parents seem to be excessively fond of all their children, male and female. A son is often spoken of playfully as a little dog,—a puppy, in fact; a girl is often spoken of as "a thousand ounces of gold," a jewel, and so forth. Sons are no doubt preferred; but is that feeling peculiar to the Chinese?

A great deal too much has been made of a passage in the *Odes*, which says that baby-sons should have sceptres to play with, while baby-daughters should have tiles.

The allotment of these toys is not quite so disparaging as it seems. The sceptre is indeed the symbol of rule; but the tile too has an honourable signification, a tile being used in ancient China as a weight for the spindle, —and consequently as a symbol of woman's work in the household.

Then, again, even a girl has a market value. Some will buy and rear them to be servants; others, to be wives for their sons; while native foundling hospitals, endowed by charitable Chinese, will actually pay a small fee for every girl handed over them.

It is also curious to note how recent careful observers have several times stated that they can find no trace of infanticide in their own immediate districts, though they hear that it is extensively practised in some other, generally distant, parts of the country.

After all, it is really a question which can be decided inferentially by statistics.

Every Chinese youth, when he reaches the age of eighteen, has a sacred duty to perform: he must marry. Broadly speaking, every adult Chinaman in the Empire has a wife; well-to-do merchants, mandarins, and others have subordinate wives, two, three, and even four. The Emperor has seventy-two. This being the case, and granting also a widespread destruction of female children, it must follow that girls are born in an overwhelmingly large proportion to boys, utterly unheard-of in any other part of the world.

Are, then, Chinese women the down-trodden, degraded creatures we used to imagine Moslem women to be?

I think this question must be answered in the negative. The young Chinese woman in a well-to-do establishment is indeed secluded, in the sense that her circle is limited to the family and to mends of the same sex.

From time immemorial it has been the rule in China that men and women should not pass things to one another,—for fear their hands might touch. A local Pharisee tried to entangle the great Mencius in his speech, asking him if a man who saw his sister-in-law drowning might venture to pull her out. "A man," replied the philosopher, "who failed to do so, would be no better than a wolf."

The Chinese lady may go out to pay calls, and even visit temples for religious purposes, unveiled, veils for women having been abolished in the first years of the seventh century of our era. Only brides wear them now.

Girls are finally separated from boys at seven or eight years of age, when the latter go to school.

Some say that Chinese girls receive no education. If so, what is the explanation of the large educational literature provided expressly for girls?

One Chinese authoress, who wrote a work on the education of women, complains that women can never expect more than ten years for their education, *i.e.* the years between childhood and marriage.

The fact is that among the literary classes girls often receive a fair education, as witness the mass of poetry published by Chinese women. One of the Dynastic Histories was partly written by a woman. Her brother, who was engaged on it, died, and she completed his work.

About the year 235 A.D., women were actually admitted to official life, and some of them rose to important government posts. By the eighth century, however, all trace of this system had disappeared.

The women of the poorer classes are not educated at all; nor indeed are the men. Both sexes have to work as burden-carriers and field labourers; and of course in such cases the restrictions mentioned above cannot be rigorously enforced.

Women of the shopkeeper class often display great aptitude for business, and render invaluable assistance to their husbands. As in France, they usually keep the cash-box.

A mandarin's seal of office is his most important possession. If he loses it, he may lose his post. Without the seal, nothing can be done; with it, everything. Extraordinary precautions are taken when transmitting new seals from Peking to the provinces. Every official seal is made with four small feet projecting from the four corners of its face, making it look like a small table. Of these, the maker breaks off one when he hands the seal over to the Board. Before forwarding to the Viceroy of the province, another foot is removed by the Board. A third is similarly disposed of by the Viceroy, and the last by the official for whose use it is intended. This is to prevent its employment by any other than the person authorised. The seal is then handed over to the mandarin's wife, in whose charge it always remains, she alone having the power to produce it, or withhold it, as required.

A Chinese woman shares the titles accorded to her husband. When the latter is promoted, the title of the wife is correspondingly advanced. She also shares all posthumous honours, and her spirit, equally with her husband's, is soothed by the ceremonies of ancestral worship.

"Ancestral worship" is a phrase of ominous import, suggesting as it does the famous dispute which began to rage early in the eighteenth century and is still raging to-day.

In every Chinese house stand small wooden tablets, bearing the names of deceased parents, grandparents, and earlier ancestors. Plates of meat and cups of wine are on certain occasions set before these tablets, in the belief that the spirits of the dead occupy the tablets and enjoy the offerings. The latter are afterward eaten by the family; but pious Chinese assert that the flavour of the food and wine has been abstracted. Similar offerings are made once a year at the tombs where the family ancestors lie buried.

The question now arises, Are these offerings set forth in the same spirit which prompts us to place flowers on graves, adorn statues, and hold memorial services?

If so, a Chinese convert to Christianity may well be permitted to embody these old observances with the ceremonial of his new faith.

Or do these observances really constitute worship? *i.e.* are the offerings made with a view to propitiate the spirits of the dead, and obtain from them increase of worldly prosperity and happiness?

In the latter case, ministers of the Christian faith would of course be justified in refusing to blend ancestral worship with the teachings of Christianity.

It would no doubt be very desirable to bring about a compromise, and discover some *modus vivendi* for the Chinese convert, other than that of throwing over Confucianism with all its influence for good, and of severing all family and social ties, and beginning life again as an outcast in his own country; but I feel bound to say that in my opinion these ancestral observances can only be regarded, strictly speaking, as worship and as nothing else.

To return to the Chinese woman. She enjoys some privileges not shared by men. She is exempt from the punishment of the bamboo, and, as a party to a case, is always more or less a source of anxiety to the presiding magistrate. No Chinaman will enter into a dispute with a woman if he can help it,—not from any chivalrous feeling, but from a conviction that he will surely be worsted in the end.

If she becomes a widow, a Chinese woman is not supposed to marry again, though in practice she very often does so. A widow who remains unmarried for thirty years may be recommended to the Throne for some mark of favour, such as an honorary tablet, or an ornamental archway, to be put up near her home. It is essential, however, that her widowhood should have begun before she was thirty years of age.

Remarriage is viewed by many widows with horror. In my own family I once employed a nurse—herself one of seven sisters—who was a widow, and who had also lost half the little finger of her left hand. The connecting link between these two details is not so apparent to us as it might be to the Chinese. After her husband's death the widow decided that she would never marry again, and in order to seal irrevocably her vow, she seized a meat-chopper and lopped off half her finger on the spot. The finger-top was placed in her husband's coffin, and the lid was closed.

This woman, who was a Christian, and the widow of a native preacher, had large, *i.e.* unbound, feet. Nevertheless, she bound the feet of her only daughter, because, as she explained, it is so difficult to get a girl married unless she has small feet.

Here we have the real obstacle to the abolition of this horrible custom, which vast numbers of intelligent Chinese would be only too glad to get rid of, if fashion did not stand in the way.

There has been in existence now for some years a well-meaning association, known as the Natural Foot Society, supported by both Chinese and foreigners, with the avowed object of putting an end to the practice of foot-binding. We hear favourable accounts of its progress; but until there is something like a national movement, it will not do to be too sanguine.

We must remember that in 1664 one of China's wisest and greatest Emperors, in the plenitude of his power issued an Imperial edict forbidding parents in future to bind the feet of their girls. Four years later the edict was withdrawn.

The Emperor was K'ang Hsi, whose name you have already heard in connection with the standard dictionary of the Chinese language and other works brought out under his patronage. A Tartar himself, unaccustomed to the sight of Tartar women struggling in such fetters, he had no sympathy with the custom; but against the Chinese people, banded together to safeguard their liberty of action in a purely domestic matter, he was quite unable to prevail.

Within the last few weeks another edict has gone forth, directed against the practice of foot-binding. Let us hope it will have a better fate.

Many years ago the prefect of T'ai-wan Fu said to me, in the course of an informal conversation after a friendly dinner, "Do you foreigners fear the inner ones?"—and on my asking what was meant, he told me that a great many Chinese stood in absolute awe of their wives. "*He* does," added the prefect, pointing to the district magistrate, a rather truculent-looking individual, who was at the dinner-party; and the other guests went into a roar of laughter.

The general statement by the prefect is borne out by the fact that the "henpecked husband" is constantly held up to ridicule in humorous literature, which would be quite impossible if there were no foundation of fact.

I have translated one of these stories, trivial enough in itself, but, like the proverbial straw, well adapted for showing which way the wind blows. Here it is:—

Ten henpecked husbands agreed to form themselves into a society for resisting the oppression of their wives. At the first meeting they were sitting talking over their pipes, when suddenly the ten wives, who had got wind of the movement, appeared on the scene.

There was a general stampede, and nine of the husbands incontinently bolted through another door, only one remaining unmoved to face the music. The ladies merely smiled contemptuously at the success of their raid, and went away.

The nine husbands them all agreed that the bold tenth man, who had not run away, should be at once appointed their president; but on coming to offer him the post, they found that he had died of fright!

To judge by the following story, the Chinese woman's patience is sometimes put to a severe test.

A scholar of old was so absent-minded, that on one occasion, when he was changing houses, he forgot to take his wife. This was reported to Confucius as a most unworthy act. "Nay," replied the Master, "it is indeed bad to forget one's wife; but 'tis worse to forget one's self!"

Points of this kind are, no doubt, trivial, as I have said above, and may be regarded by many even as flippant; but the fact is that a successful study of the Chinese people cannot possibly be confined to their classics and higher literature, and to the problem of their origin and subsequent development where we now find them. It must embrace the lesser, not to say meaner, details of their everyday life, if we are ever to pierce the mystery which still to a great extent surrounds them.

In this sense an Italian student of Chinese, Baron Vitale, has gone so far as to put together and publish a collection of Chinese nursery rhymes, from which it is not difficult to infer that Chinese babies are very much as other babies are in other parts of the world.

And it has always seemed to me that the Chinese baby's father and mother, so far as the ordinary springs of action go, are very much of a pattern with the rest of mankind.

One reason why the Chinaman remains a mystery to so many is due, no doubt, to the vast amount of nonsense which is published about him.

First of all, China is a very large country, and from want of proper means of communication for many centuries, there has been nothing like extensive intercourse between North, South, East, West, and Central. Of course the officials visit all parts of the Empire, as they are transferred from post to post; but the bulk of the people never get far beyond the range of their own district city.

The consequence is that as regards manners and customs, while retaining an indelible national imprint, the Chinese people have drifted apart into separate local communities; so that what is true of one part of the country is by no means necessarily true of another.

The Chinese themselves say that manners, which they think are due to climatic influences, change every thirty miles; customs, which they attribute to local idiosyncrasies, change every three hundred miles.

Now, a globe-trotter goes to Canton, and as one of the sights of that huge collection of human beings, he is taken to shops,—there used to be three,—where the flesh of dogs, fed for the purpose, is sold as food.

He comes home, and writes a book, and says that the Chinese people live on dogs' flesh.

When I was a boy, I thought that every Frenchman had a frog for breakfast. Each statement would be about equally true. In the north of China, dogs' flesh is unknown; and even in the south, during all my years in China I never succeeded in finding any Chinaman who either could, or would, admit that he had actually tasted it.

Take the random statement that any rich man condemned to death can procure a substitute by payment of so much. So long as we believe stuff of that kind, so long will the Chinese remain a mystery for us, it being difficult to deduce true conclusions from false premises.

As a matter of fact, that is, so far as my own observations go, the Chinese people value life every whit as highly as we do, and a substitute of the kind would be quite unprocurable under ordinary circumstances. It is thinkable that some poor wretch, himself under sentence of death, might be substituted with the connivance of the officials, to hoodwink foreigners; but even then the difficulties would be so great as to render the scheme almost impracticable.

For in China everything leaks out. There is none of that secrecy necessary to conceal and carry out such a plot.

At any rate, the uncertainty which gathers around many of these points emphasises the necessity of more and more accurate scholarship in Chinese, and more and more accurate information on the people of China and their ways.

How the latter article is supplied to us in England, you may judge from some extracts which I have recently taken from respectable daily and weekly newspapers.

For instance, "China has only one hundred physicians to a population of four hundred millions."

To me it is inconceivable how such rubbish can be printed, especially when it is quite easy to find out that there is no medical diploma in China, and that any man who chooses is free to set up as a doctor.

By a pleasant fiction, he charges no fees; a fixed sum, however, is paid to him for each visit, as "horse-money,"—I need hardly add, in advance.

There are, as with us, many successful, and consequently fashionable, doctors whose "horse-money" runs well into double figures. Their success must be due more to good luck and strictly innocent prescriptions than to any guidance they can find in the extensive medical literature of China.

All together, medicine is a somewhat risky profession, as failure to cure is occasionally resented by surviving relatives.

There is a story of a doctor who had mismanaged a case, and was seized by the patient's family and tied up. In the night he managed to free himself, and escaped by swimming across a river. When he got home, he found his son, who had just begun to study medicine, and he said to him, "Don't be in a hurry with your books; the first and most important thing is to learn to swim!"

Here is another newspaper gem: "In China, the land of opposites, the dials of the clocks are made to turn round, while the hands stand still."

Personally, I never noticed this arrangement.

Again: "Some of the tops with which the Chinese amuse themselves are as large as barrels. It takes three men to spin one, and it gives off a sound that may be heard several hundred yards away."

"The Chinese National Anthem is so long that it takes half a day to sing it."

"Chinese women devote very little superfluous time to hair-dressing. Their tresses are arranged once a month, and they sleep with their heads in boxes."

What we want in place of all this is a serious and systematic examination of the manners and customs, and modes of thought, of the Chinese people.

Their long line of Dynastic Histories must be explored and their literature ransacked by students who have got through the early years of drudgery inseparable from the peculiar nature of the written language, and who are prepared to devote themselves, not, as we do now, to a general knowledge of the whole, but to a thorough acquaintance with some particular branch.

The immediate advantages of such a course, as I must point out once more, for the last time, to commerce and to diplomatic relations will be incalculable. And they will be shared in by the student of history, philosophy, and religion, who will then for the first time be able to assign to China her proper place in the family of nations.

The founder of this Chinese Chair has placed these advantages within the grasp of Columbia University.

www.ingramcontent.com/pod-product-compliance
Lightning Source LLC
Chambersburg PA
CBHW080909190726
48294CB00008B/2025